Truth or Trigger

How Falling in Love with Your Ego Connects You with Your Soul

By Catherine Graham

Other Titles by Catherine Graham

Woman to Woman, the Journey to Me
Power Surge
A Journey into Fear
Naked Soul

Oracle Decks by Catherine Graham

Bitchslaps from the Universe
Journey Within
Journey the Fuck Within
Soulgasms (coming 2021)

Copyright © 2021 by Catherine Graham

Printed in the United States by lulupress.com. Distributed in Canada by Journey Healers. www.journeyhealers.com

Cover Photo by Canva.com

All rights reserved. No part of this book may be reproduced by any mechanical, photographic, or electronic process or in the form of phonographic recording, nor may it be stored in a retrieval system, transmitted or otherwise be copied for public or private use- other than for 'fair use' as brief quotations embodied in articles and reviews- without prior permission of the author.

The author of this book does not dispense medical advice or prescribe the use of any technique as a form of treatment for physical, emotional, medical problems without the advice of a physician, either directly or indirectly. The intent of the author is only to offer information of a general nature to help you in your quest of emotional and spiritual wellbeing. In the event you use any of the information in this book for yourself, which is your constitutional right, the author assumes no responsibility for your actions.

Graham, Catherine

Truth or Trigger: How Falling in Love with Your Ego Connects You with Your Soul
ISBN 978-1-716-18905-0

1st Printing 2021
Printed in the United States of America by lulupress.com

Dedicated to:

All of the Wounded Inner Children of the World

May we recognize them, soothe them, heal them and love them.

Foreward (Before You Begin)

"If you want to do any healing work, you must first rid yourself of the ego" a spiritual friend said to me one day, after I had expressed to her some frustration over a family matter.

I felt gutted.

There was that damn ego again. I had heard it before, and I was sure I would hear it again.

No matter how good I was, no matter how much healing work I did, it all kept coming back to the fact that I had this damn thing called an 'ego' and I had to get rid of it.

All of my outer experiences, all of the emotions I was feeling, all of my relationships (and the issues) kept stemming back to the Ego. Every spiritual person, healer and teacher I had kept claiming it to be.

I wouldn't have this problem if I didn't have an Ego.

I wouldn't have been triggered I would simply let go of my Ego.

I wouldn't feel fearful if I could stash the Ego away somewhere.

They were all trying to be helpful, and yet, it seemed as though I was caught in a tailspin trying to get this whole spirituality thing to work right for me, without the dreaded Ego attached.

Outwardly I would smile, and nod, and agree with them. Yes, this damn Ego.

Inside, I hurt. I felt ashamed. Why couldn't I get it right? What was wrong with me? What the hell was the secret to all of this? What was it that I was doing wrong? Did the Universe have it out for me, as it was so easily ridding everyone else of their Ego, and mine was stuck to me like a fly to a glue strip?

Then came the anger. The anger at myself for not getting it perfected yet, for still feeling all of the human emotions and not being able to let them go the way everyone else thought I should.

Jealousy at those who were completely ego-less in their existence.

Embarrassment at the Ego within me that stayed around.

I felt it all. And I carried it with me.

To the outside world, I had it together. I could fake the 'ego-less' part of me. I could smile when triggered, I could push down the emotions, and I could brace myself through the fears. I could be the 'ego-less spiritual leader' that I was told to be; the good daughter that didn't break the rules; the mom and step-mom that kept her cool; the friend that didn't require a dual relationship; the wife that didn't complain.

Until I couldn't.

And then the anger, frustration, resentment and jealousy would all rear their ugly heads (again), and I was left feeling embarrassed and ashamed (again) for still not figuring this out.

And that was when I realized I needed to change. Not for them, not for anyone really, but for myself.

If you're reading this, chances are, you, like me, have been living your life trying to please everyone but yourself; trying to act selfless rather than selfish; and feeling a bit burnt out by showing up for everyone except for yourself.

The following pages are my own experience with creating a loving relationship with my Ego, to help me connect to the truth of who I am. Take what resonates, leave what doesn't.

After all, as much as it's about me finding my truth, it's just as much about you finding your truth as well. This is the journey back to you- all of you- not just the bits that society, your parents, your partners, your friends, or your children accept; this is the return to all of you... the good, the bad, and everything in between.

Welcome.

You're in my tribe now.

With love,

Catherine

Chapter #1

My Ego Has a First Name

Ego. It has gotten such a bad rap over the years, especially in the days of new age spiritual enlightenment hitting the mass markets. When I first started down the path of spiritual awakening, it was learned very quickly that my Ego was something that I should be working on getting rid of, and fast.

The problem was that I wasn't exactly sure how I could get rid of this thing called the ego. Whenever I would hear the inner voice coming up that was telling me I was better than, or worse than, I would be filled with a shame so deep. I still had that Ego thing lurking around. And I just couldn't seem to shake it.

And yet, the big spiritual gurus would make comments about the Ego being fear driven, the Ego taking you away from your own spiritual essence, the Ego being the drive behind greed, selfishness and dishonesty.

Ugh.

Knowing that I wanted this spiritual enlightenment thing more so than anything else, I set out to get rid of it once and for all.

Given the fact that I was so shame-filled about this ego thing, I found it difficult to put into words when working with spiritual masters and enlightened ones what it was that I was seeking.

They all claimed to have no ego, to be working from a place of the heart, to be enlightened and all-knowing.

I would compare myself, and what I was able to do, versus everything that they were doing. It seemed they had a much better idea as to what was happening than what I ever would.

Oh, my ego was a strong one.

And while I see myself as being quite knowledgeable about the ego, and the role it now plays, I will also let you know that I am no expert. I have years of experience in working with this strong force within me, however, I lack the book smarts that some are hoping for when it comes to the world of self-help books and experts. I could read a bunch of books about the ego, and throw some psychological bull at you about the role the ego plays in a way that I was able to understand it, however, I do believe experience to be the best teacher.

So, my experience:

My husband and I went to Los Angeles to a transformational weekend with speaker and comedian, Kyle Cease. In my mind, I imagined the best things possible. I would be called up on the stage, Kyle would notice me, I would talk about my work, and the world would fall in love with me.

That wasn't the way it worked though at any level.

When we first arrived to Los Angeles, we were both feeling the thrill of being in a new city to explore, and excited for everything that was about to transpire.

On the first day of the event, I found myself feeling very teary eyed. Something deep was shifting inside of me, and being the type of person who tries to keep it all together for everyone else, I was doing everything that I could to keep it together.

By our lunch break on the first day of the workshop, I felt my heart pounding heavy in my chest. No matter how

I tried to stop the feelings that were coming up, they were coming up, and not in a very gentle way at all.

On our way back from lunch, a homeless person stepped in front of me. Now, in my city, we have homeless people. I am not ignorant to this fact. However, the man in front of me was like nothing I had ever experienced in my life before. In fact, he made the homeless in my own city look like they were quite privileged.

His hair was matted to his head with dirt and debris, his clothes, old and worn, with holes and hanging off his frail body. His shoes, about 2 sizes too small for his feet, displayed bloody, blistered and cracked heels.

How do we let people live like that? Why doesn't anyone care about him? Why has he been so abandoned? Why doesn't he choose differently? Why isn't anyone helping him?

My tears blurred by eyes, and I felt a lump in my throat. My mind raced on, but there was another story that was coming up… an experience I had buried years before.

I was fifteen when we found out my father had cancer. Within a week of getting the news from the doctor, he had three tumors removed from his brain. Within six months, he had completed chemotherapy and radiation, and still the news was grim. He would be dead within a year.

Now for some, the idea of losing a parent is devastating. It is something that makes people connect deeper with each other, and want to spend more time with one another.

For my fifteen year old self though, I was angry. I was pissed off that he was dying. I was pissed off that he wasn't choosing differently. I was mad that I was now needing to miss out on things because he was sick.

At first I displayed this through angry outbursts, and

breaking the rules that my parents had set out for me. I tried to slit my wrists, I tried to overdose on Tylenol and birth control. It seemed though that God didn't want me to die just yet though, as nothing seemed to be working.

A friend and I decided that we were both tired of what our parents were choosing and so we made plans to leave the country. We were going to travel to Los Angeles, and she would become a stripper, and I would become a porn star.

While this is laughable to my adult self, as a child, I felt it was the best option given the circumstances that I was needing to face.

Luckily for both of us, her mother's credit card wouldn't work, and we were unable to purchase the airplane tickets to Los Angeles, so we had to stay put.

My father died 4 months later, surrounded by his four daughters, his wife, his siblings and his parents. It was my first 'face to face' with death, and one that was etched into my mind.

The lead up to his death though was something that I had hidden away in the corners of my mind. The pain, the anger, the frustration, the grief. I had hidden it for so long, being the 'strong one', being the 'one who keeps it altogether' that I forgot it was there in the first place.

And it was the homeless man walking in front of me on Hollywood Boulevard that brought it all back up to the surface, for me to see and feel in a very real way that I was unable to do in my younger years.

I didn't recognize it at first. In fact, I told my husband who was looking at me questionably that I was simply being 'empathic' to what the homeless man was feeling, and that was the cause of my tears.

Thankfully, my husband, on the same journey as me, was able to hold the space for me, while asking the right questions so that we could get to the truth of it all.

"What are you feeling exactly?" Jon asked me.

"I just feel like he was so alone and nobody loves him, and it's like the world is so fucked... how do we let people live like that?" I cried to him.

"Okay, so are you feeling his feelings or are you feeling your own feelings?" he gently prodded.

I glared at him, with the tears streaming down my face. I wanted it to be about the homeless man, but all I kept coming back to was the fact that if I had followed through with my fifteen year old plans of moving to L.A, I very easily could have been the homeless person.

I relented. "I am feeling my own feelings." The tears came harder now, and the lump that had been building in my throat exploded. "I just remember how alone I was. I remember feeling like I had nobody. And it's like my whole damn life, I have been alone. Like nobody loves me or supports me, and that homeless guy... that's what he's feeling now too".

I cried, and cried, and cried some more. It was like waves of everything that I had been holding onto for so damn long finally released, and now there was no holding back.

"Is that your ego talking, or your heart talking?" Jon then asked.

Again, I glared at him.

"I'm always alone," I retorted.

"Is that your truth, or is that your Ego talking?" he prodded.

The best thing about doing transformational weekends as a couple is that you're growing and learning as a couple. The worst thing about doing transformational weekends as a couple is that your partner is in a 'mode' where they are willing and ready to help you see past your own internal bullshit.

I sighed. "It's my Ego". The truth was, I was never truly alone. I knew that at some level, but at this level that I was at in this moment, it felt that every time I really truly needed someone, I was left to my own defenses and that I was truly alone.

"Would you like me to start pointing out to you every time your Ego is running the show?" Jon then asked me, half joking and half serious.

It felt like a lightbulb moment to me.

"Ummm... yah!?" I told him, grabbing a coke from the hotel fridge.

He replied with a giant 'EGO' reverberating through the room.

Looking at my coke, I noticed the name 'Kevin' on the side, asking me to share a coke with 'Kevin'.

I showed Jon the coke, and said, 'Maybe we can call my ego Kevin'.

Then Jon yelled, louder than before, "KEEEVVVIIIN!!!!!!"

I laughed, and then cried again. "That sounded just like the mom on Home Alone when she realizes she forgot about Kevin.... and he was abandoned to." More tears, more I named my ego Kevin, and that was the day I started my journey in falling in love with my ego, so I could connect deeper with my heart.

Now, I understand that giving your ego a first name may seem a bit strange to some, and for others, I promise, I don't have split personalities or a multiple personality disorder (although if you do, that's okay too!).

The idea of naming my ego gave me a starting point

to start to understand why and how it was showing up in my life, rather than bashing it into the ground or trying to get rid of it completely.

In that weekend, I realized that my ego was not something to be feared, embarrassed by, or ashamed of.

To me, through the naming of Kevin, I was able to differentiate what was my heart speaking and what was my ego that was speaking. I was able to see where my ego would hold me back from truly living my best life and where my ego was being triggered by something in the past.

At first, I would refer to Kevin as 'fucking Kevin' and roll my eyes at the fact that he was showing up again, was being triggered again, and was still, to my dismay, existing. I made jokes about Kevin and laughed at the expense of myself and my hurting inner self.

And yet, over time, I was able to see the hurt and pain that Kevin had experienced, and in all of the ways that Kevin had felt lost and abandoned. The ego here wasn't the bad guy. The ego was the part of me that felt alone, ashamed, abandoned, lost, confused and angry.

In my plight to 'get rid of the ego' I only emphasized everything that the ego had already experienced. The more the ego was showing itself to me, the more frustrated I would become and neglect everything that it was presenting to me. What it was truly needing though was an opportunity to be loved, an opportunity to be seen, and heard and validated in the pain that it had experienced.

And so the journey of 'getting rid of the ego' became the journey of fully loving and understanding all of the parts of me that didn't have the space to be seen, loved, heard or validated in the past. And that was where the true growth began to happen.

The ego was designed to keep us safe. Back in the

times of the cavemen, the ego was the part of the brain that would send off the alarm signal that there was a tiger hiding behind the bush, and that we needed to run, or fake our own death. It made sense back then. It was survival.

But as we have grown and adapted, we typically don't have encounters with tigers anymore.

Now though, our tigers have become something worst: The experiences that have molded and shaped us into believing that we are not enough, that we are not loved, that we are in danger if we do the things that our heart wants, that we will not have enough money, that we are surrounded with death and things to fear, more so than ever before.

We live in a day and age where we have more answers at our fingertips, we can stream information from so many sources, and our possibilities are endless.

And yet, we are all suffering at the same time. Suffering in our own internal pain, suffering in believing that we aren't good enough, or will ever be enough. We watch the news and think everything is doom and gloom (Here's a hint: Stop watching the news!)

In our plight to reach spiritual enlightenment, we have neglected the piece of ourselves that has been hurt in the past, and that's just needing a bit of the spotlight so that it can heal once and for all.

Many of us have been taught to spiritually by-pass any and all negative emotions that come up, or we will not be worthy enough to reach the 'golden light'.

I was a great spiritual by-passer. I would fake the love and light, and keep my head held high as I moved from one lesson to the next, always using my mind to focus on what I was taught, rather than tapping into my heart, and my body to truly feel what was coming up for me.

The more I began to sit in silence with Kevin, the

more I was able to realize how much I had been trying to keep everything together for so long, and quite frankly, I was so fucking tired of keeping up with it all.

Every day, I would show up to sit with Kevin. Like a meditation with a purpose, I simply would sit, and observe what it was my ego needed to say that day. Some days were easier than others. Some days I wanted to tell the inner voice to shut the hell up so I could reach some level of inner peace. Other days, I was able to simply observe the thoughts that were coming up and the feelings that were connected to them. And then, Kevin and I would just sit. Not working on fixing anything, or being anything other than what we were. Hurting, fearful, apprehensive and angry.

A Dream about Kevin- July 2018

My husband and I had just bought a house, and we took our kids to go and see it. When we got there, the real estate woman turned around and looked at us. She looked like a woman from the 80's, with her bright clothes, pink lipstick and poufy blonde hair. At the time of the dream, I had not watched Schitt's Creek, however, now having it on my watch list, and looking back, she looked a lot like Jocelyn from the show.

"Oh you're finally here! I am so excited!" she exclaimed to us. "Would you like to see the house?"

We nodded, and started to walk through the house, which, while it looked decent from the outside, the inside was quite a mess. There was garbage everywhere, old soiled laundry laying around, and not necessarily what one might be excited to be moving into.

We saw a pool in the backyard, and even though the water was greener than blue or clear, the kids all happily jumped in and started to swim around.

"Would you like to see the bedroom?" the woman asked.

We nodded in agreement and followed her down a hallway, and into what looked like a bathroom. There was a red toilet, and a red bathtub. The toilet was filled to the brim with feces. The bathtub was dirty, and blankets inside created a makeshift bed.

"This is the bedroom?" I asked, a bit disturbed by the condition of it.

"Well, yes, it's 'Kevin's room'" she explained to me. "It's no wonder he's angry, look at what he's living in!"

A Dream about Kevin- July 2018

I was in a high school gym, watching a wrestling tournament. Two young men were wrestling, but one was getting particularly angry about the match. He took out a cylinder block. He placed in on the other young man's neck.

I grabbed him and pulled him to the side, yelling, 'What are you doing? You are going to hurt someone if you don't control yourself!'

He dropped down against the hard wall, looked up at me and said, 'Well you hurt me all the time'.

I asked him what he meant.

'Telling me to shut up and shit. You can be downright mean. I just need you to listen.'

I sat down beside him. 'Oh' was all I could reply.

'I'm Kevin, by the way' he said as he reached out his hand to me.

'Kevin? Really? I'm trying to know you!'

'Well now you do' he said and walked away.

The dreams were profound. As much as I had been sitting with Kevin, for the first time, I was being invited into the world of my ego, where I was able to see the neglect and dirtiness that I had created for it. In my journey to being 'spiritually enlightened' I had created this awful space for my ego to live in.

In my dream world, I knew from previous experiences that the dream was representing my psyche, and as much as I had built up new houses in the past, I had yet to build a house for my Ego, and from the state of the house I was being shown I was going to have to start at the very beginning, cleaning up the shit, getting rid of the dirty laundry, and finding a bed in there somewhere so my Ego could get the rest it needed.

My meditation that day was different. I didn't just sit with Kevin and let the thoughts come up and be observed.

On this day, I simply stated to Kevin, 'I am so sorry I have been neglecting you. I am so sorry that your living conditions have been so horrendous. I will do better."

That meditation was one of the most beautiful to date. Rather than my mind running overtime, I found myself sinking deeper and deeper into this 'knowing' that I was okay, that I was safe, and that I was truly loved and supported by something greater than I was able to see.

That was the day that Kevin and I forged a friendship, a new way of living and co-existing in a world that had often left us alone to fend for ourselves. That was the day that I found my way back to my heart and began a deeper healing journey than I had experienced to date.

Chapter #2

A Chance to Be Loved

Simply calling my ego Kevin wasn't enough to change the course of how much my ego was dictating my life. While it gave me an opportunity to see where the ego was leading versus the heart was leading, there was still a lot of learning and unlearning that I was needing to go through.

It would be easy for me to place the blame on my parents, on school teachers and others in my life who had put me down, abandoned me, or left me to my own defenses. It would be easy for me to look at the disappointments of life, and say, I am this way because of this, and leave it at that, without giving myself a chance for growth or forgiveness.

However, I had already functioned that way, and I was honestly tired of it. It felt like this revolving door that I just couldn't get out of. I had to do things differently.

What I began to realize was that the ways that I had been treated throughout my life was the way I treated my ego. With disgust, with shame, with anger and resentment. Whenever the ego would act up I wanted it to shut the hell up, get over it, and move on.

I had to change the way I was talking to it and listening to it.

It took some convincing (meditation, really) for me to have the conversations with Kevin that would eventually pull him out of the bathroom that I had discarded him in.

I had to become the safe space for my ego to come out and show itself to me, and see that it was safe to do so in my body.

I began to see Kevin as not only this 15 year old kid that was pissed off at the world, but also as the three year old child who was molested, the six year old child who was lonely, the twelve year old child who was bullied.

And the more I began to recognize these lost parts of myself, and seeing them as the little kids that they were, the more love and compassion I began to hold for them.

You see, our ego is developing as we grow and learn and become functioning adults. It is formed by the scraped knees when we run too fast, and become the voice that tells us to slow down next time. It is formed by the oral presentation we have to give in front of our class, and when we slip on the words, it becomes the voice that tells us we can't speak out in public settings.

Every experience, whether we see it as good or bad, becomes the voice of the ego.

Most often, we have these experiences at a time when we are so little and emotionally immature, that we are unable to fully process what we have felt, and what has happened. The ego helps us out here too, and does it's best to prevent us from feeling those big feelings in all future events, while also filling in any gaps in the story to be sure that we will be safe the next time around.

For myself, one of these ego stories was that I couldn't ask for help from anyone. In my body, the thought of asking for help really gave me anxiety. I didn't like to rely on anyone else, I didn't want to be a burden for anyone else, and honestly, I felt that asking for help would surely hurt me in some way or another.

For my husband, this was exasperating. He would watch me go from being a completely independent and sure of herself woman, to a bubbling crying mess at the thought of asking anyone for help with anything.

This really came to light one night when our vehicle broke down and I was unable to drive our kids to their football practice. One of the other moms and I had done trades in the past, where I would drive them there, and she would drive them home. On this day though, I couldn't drive. I was devastated and scared about how angry she must be that I wasn't able to. I couldn't even message her to ask if she would be able to. I made my husband do it, and even as he did, my hands were shaking at what her reaction would be.

    I couldn't explain the fear to anyone, let alone myself. All I knew was that I hated to ask for help. This mom gladly took the boys to their football practice and brought them home, wishing us good luck with our broken vehicle. Her reaction did not match the story that my ego was telling me would surely happen.

    The following week, while on a meditation retreat, the experience was completely out of my mind. On the last day of the retreat, during our last meditation of the day, I was taken back to when I was two or three years old.

*   My sister and I were playing ring around the rosy on our cement pad deck with some other kids. We were being babysat by our next door neighbor and her husband. It was sunny. I was wearing a white dress.*
*   I had to use the bathroom.*
*   I asked.*
*   Eric, the neighbor's husband took me by the hand and into the house.*
*   A baby was playing in the playpen in the living room and looked at us when we went into the house.*
*   We went into the bathroom and I went pee.*
*   And then Eric proceeded to molest me. He touched me, and put his penis in my mouth.*

Don't ask for help. You will be hurt if you do. Don't ask for help. It's not safe. Don't ask for help.
The words kept repeating in my mind.

Tears streamed down my face, and I stayed there in my mind, with this broken and hurt part of myself that was hurt so badly by asking for help.

Rather than telling myself to 'get over it', or that 'it was silly to react that way', I simply placed my hands on my heart, and started to speak gently to myself, *'Thank you for keeping me safe. I will protect you. You are safe with me. You are loved for feeling scared in my body. You are loved for being afraid to ask for help. You don't have to do this alone. Together we will ask for help. I will protect you'.*

And with that, the fearful voice within became calm. The part of me that so wanted to hide and escape the pain breathed a sigh of relief.

I became the space that I needed when I was a child to feel the big feelings. I became the parent to my ego in that moment, in a big way, to validate the ego's experience, while also grabbing it by the hand to say, 'that is what we have done in the past, and that's okay, but now, let me show you a better way'.

Seeing my ego as these broken parts of myself gave me the opportunity to give and receive love for myself in a way that I hadn't allowed myself to in the past.

For many of us, when it comes to the inner self talk, we are cruel. We are bullies. In fact, if we are asked to say those words out loud to a friend, or to a loved one, we would be too ashamed to do so.

But when it comes to ourselves and the way that we speak to ourselves, and all of those inner children within us, everything is game.

In one workshop that I taught, I asked the women to

write down the most repeated words that play in their minds.

The ramblings were different: *You are too fat. You are not worthy. You are not enough. Don't speak up. You should be ashamed of yourself. You're ugly. You're stupid.* But the messages were all the same.

I then pulled out a premade picture board with pictures of my kids, my nieces, and my great nieces. One by one, I placed the woman's words as speech bubbles coming out of the pictures, as though these were the words that the child was speaking.

Seeing the words pictured like that had many of the women breaking down in tears.

"It's awful to see that a child could feel that way. I just want to reach into the picture and give her a hug" one woman told me.

They were her words. She was only able to see the cruelty of the words when she was attached them to a child saying them and believing them about themselves.

Many of us are able to see children as being the way of the future, and when it comes to raising them, inspiring them and helping them, we all have ideas on what is the best way to do so.

One common theme between all of us though is that we need to make these children feel loved.

If a child was to come to us to tell us they thought they were stupid, we surely wouldn't agree with them. We may ask them why they think that way, and then hear them out. Then we may point out all of the ways that they have been smart, and affirm to them how much we love them. Not once would we look at the child and tell them to shut up, get over it, or that they were right for feeling the way that they were.

In fact, just the idea of doing it is horrendous for us.

So why then, do we do this to ourselves?

For every thought that these women wrote down, there was a strong childhood experience that created those words. And now it was so engrained in their mind, that they weren't able to remember a time in their life when they didn't feel that way or say those things about themselves.

Looking at the ego as this young child beside you, rather than this thing that you have to overcome or get rid of, gives you the chance to start to heal the inner child from the experiences that made it feel so hurt in the first place.

In that, you can start by giving your ego a chance to be loved by you. While our parents, our caregivers, our teachers, and others that we looked at to help shape our way may not have lead us down a path of trusting and believing in ourselves, it doesn't mean that we have to continue to live that way. Again, this is not a blaming game, but rather, an understanding and awareness that the adults we had in our lives may not have had access to any information that would allow them to choose differently.

But the fact that you're reading this book right now, tells me that you're ready to access a new type of information and to use it to create a different reality in your relationship with yourself.

When you are able to see your ego as this part of you that was developed when you were five, eight or nineteen, that was too hurt, too scared or too angry to be able to move through and process the experience, you begin to separate the 'you' that you were before the experience, and the 'you' you became during and after the experience.

Often, people talk about someone showing their 'true colors' when they make a mistake, or act in a way that is dishonest or cruel.

However, I have yet to meet a newborn baby who is

ready to commit a crime, let someone down or be rude or cruel for the sake of being rude or cruel.

Our true colors have never been about putting ourselves or others down, hurting ourselves or hurting others. Our true colors are pure love. Our true colors are seeing beyond the physical appearance of others, the physical appearance of ourselves, and trusting in the feeling that a person brings forward.

It is through painful experiences that we begin to lose sight of our true colors, and the true colors of others, and in that we begin to separate ourselves from the oneness that we are, and the inherent greatness that we all have.

It is through these painful experiences that our egos are born, and start slaving away to stop us from experiencing the pain again.

In essence, the ego is the manifestation of the disconnect between who we truly are in our hearts and soul, and what our experiences have taught us we are in our minds. It is in this separation that we begin to lose our connection from the Source energy that we are, and begin to fill ourselves with thoughts and feelings of being alone, afraid, doomed and separate from one another.

Because our parents and caregivers didn't have the tools to help us through these experiences (or used the best tools that they had in the best way that they could), it is our jobs now, as the adult-self to give the child-self and ego-voice a chance to be loved.

The adult-self will 'explain away' the experience, through the lens of the adult-eyes. Our minds seek to figure out why this experience happened, what lessons needed to be learned, why certain behaviors come from certain people, etc.

The child-self and ego-voice don't need an

explanation though. The child-self and ego-voice just simply need to be loved for all of the big feelings that are being experienced.

In the case of myself, and my absolute fear of asking for help, I didn't need to know 'why' I was afraid to ask for help. I didn't need the logistics of it all, nor did I need to explain to my younger self why that certain experience didn't mean that I couldn't ask for help.

What Kevin (child-self/ego-voice) needed to hear was love. It needed to hear that it was perfectly fine that asking for help felt scary. It needed to know that it was loved even when it didn't want to ask for help. It needed to feel loved for feeling fearful, it needed to feel loved for being hurt and it needed to feel loved for being angry about a situation that was completely out of its control.

In doing that, the part of me that felt it was unworthy of love for having such feelings, suddenly felt safe and loved as it was. It no longer had 'something to prove' to the world. It was simply enough.

Heart Work:

When you feel emotions coming up for you, place your hands on your heart and tell yourself that it's totally okay for you to feel that way. Tell yourself that you will love yourself no matter what you are feeling.

Example:

You are feeling angry about a recent conversation with a friend. Rather than telling yourself to get over it, put your hands on your heart and say to yourself:

"You have a right to be angry in my body. I love you for feeling angry. I love you for wanting to defend yourself. I love you for all that you are showing me right now.

Chapter # 3

Triggered

I started to write this book in 2018, and am nearing the finish line of it in late 2020. Anyone alive in 2020 knows what a shitshow of a year it has been, highlighted by a global pandemic, a presidential election like I've never seen before, huge protects for social justice for black lives, and an overly-divided world, creating the perfect platform on social media for fighting, name-calling, and cancel culture.

There have been days when I have had to put my cell phone away and stay off of social media sites as the bombardment of division felt too heavy for me to be able to deal with.

Rather than having conversations to understand the story on the other side of opinion online, there have been many caught up in 'outing' people, in arguing, in breaking up relationships, families, and more.

There are those who believe in the pandemic, and those who believe it's all a conspiracy. There are those who support Black Lives Matter, and those who believe that All Lives Matter. There are those who believe Trump is the best president ever (whether they are American or not) and those who believe Biden is the only one who can bring forward healing for the USA (whether they are American or not). At this very moment, the greatest of arguments seems to stem around the wearing or not wearing of masks, and getting the vaccine or not getting the vaccine.

In a world where oneness is trying to be achieved, all we are creating is more division and separation.

My daughter had a class throughout all of this for civics and careers, where a large aspect of the civics part of the course was to decide what political view you had, and debate as to why you believed what you believed. The topics up for debate were abortions, and the mask issue of Covid19.

My daughter, being 15 years old, a Gemini, and not one for conflict had the opinion that 'both sides are correct', which the teacher promptly put down. He told her she had to either be pro-abortion or anti-abortion; pro-mask or anti-mask. She wasn't able to be in the middle and see both sides of view.

For myself, I believed that seeing both sides was an opinion, and supported my daughter in this belief.

I got an email from the teacher, who felt obliged to tell me that her participation in the class due to her inability to form an opinion was going to earn her a lesser mark. At first I thought it was a joke, and then realized that this is the society that we are living in right now.

We are all told to have opinions. To be on one side or the other. We can't be in between. In the example of my daughter's class, it was have an opinion with an opposing side, or you will get less.

The problem with opinions is that they are based on experience and the perception that comes from that experience. And yet, we all stand so convicted that our opinion is the highest form of truth that there is. We allow what triggers us to be the basis of this, and in that, react from the trigger point, rather than a space of love and openness.

This year especially, it seems as though anyone who has a different perception than our own is seen as a threat, and so we react accordingly, trying to keep ourselves as safe as possible. And yet, we are all only adding to the division of the world, and ultimately, the division of ourselves at the core.

When we stop ourselves from being open and willing to listen to another's point of view, or experience, we ultimately are telling ourselves, and our inner child, and earlier experiences that anything that we don't 'approve of' must be banished and never to be heard from again.

Last week, while stepping in to co-lead a workshop, the organizer and I got on the conversation of 2020, and all of the triggers and traumas that were happening.

He told me that at the beginning of the pandemic, he had been in meditation, and was shown an eagle, flying high above the clouds, taking everything in, absorbing it all. The eagle represented both sides of opinions, as the eagle was unable to fly with just the left wing, or just the right wing. He needed both to be able to balance on the winds. When balance was achieved, the eagle was able to soar higher, seeing a broader view, and connecting closer to the Universe from the higher view point.

We need both the light and the dark, the ego and the soul, the right and the wrong, the black and the white, the birth and the death for our balance. Too much light and we get burnt, too much darkness and we feel depressed and disconnected.

The same is true with our opinions. We need to hear them all, to experience them all, even if done as a witness to someone else's experience.

One interesting thing about me is that I love to eat orange popsicles in a hot shower, in the middle of a Canadian winter. The heat from the shower makes the popsicle soften and sweat just like it does in the heat of the summer, and can transport me to warm sunny days in my mind very quickly.

Most people when they hear this will say one of a few phrases: (Laughing) that's weird.... But maybe I should try it! I'm totally doing that when I go home; Ew, I would never eat in the shower.

Of all of the people that I've told this to, no one has ever been triggered into cancelling their relationship with me, even if they do think I may be a bit weird for it.

The reason for this?

My love for orange popsicles in the shower isn't a threat to them, or their feeling of safety and security.

It's the same for those who like pineapple on pizza (me!), those who prefer beer over wine, or listening to rock and roll music rather than country.

These small differences in our society are celebrated, and often met with a 'try it once before you decide' kind of attitude.

And yet the bigger differences, and the 'real life' issues that we are experiencing, our triggers become more about what we believe is going to keep us safest, and we begin to see everyone else as a threat

I want to also point out here that I am in no way talking about triggers from physical, sexual or mental and emotional abuse, nor those associated with PTSD. As I have said earlier in this book, I am not a therapist, nor do I have a doctorate degree in trauma. When I speak of triggers, I am talking about the general nuances of life that send us into a tailspin of emotions.

Everyone has an opinion. Some may differ than the one that you have and that's okay.

Everyone has a trigger (or multiple). Some may have triggers that are similar to your own and will fight alongside you to abolish the trigger. Some may look at your trigger and say it's not that big of a deal because they don't experience it the same way that you do. And that's okay too.

Everyone has the ability to be the toxic person, and

everyone has the ability to be the person affected by the toxic person.

In our society, trigger points are noted as a reason to stop a relationship, stop a conversation, label someone as toxic, and resent what brought the trigger on in the first place.

This is where we can all learn to do better, to be better.

We have become so afraid to be hurt, to be offended, and to feel uncomfortable in any way, and so we avoid all triggers at all costs, in order to keep us the most comfortable.

We talk about helicopter parents who watch their kids too closely, we talk about the snowflake generation that is so offended by everything, and we talk about toxic people like everyone is oozing poison.

And yet, we have become our own helicopter parents… avoiding danger or being triggered at all costs, to make sure we can stay as comfortable as possible. We are the ones who say, I am so offended, or get offended by someone else being offended. We may even avoid conversations that have controversy in order to protect our uncomfortable feelings from coming forward. We are the toxic people, allowing ourselves to walk around with all of our triggers buried deep inside of us, oozing out our own poison, and hoping like hell that no one will show them to us.

A few years ago, I had a really painful shoulder. It was burning constantly, and I would often have Jon dig his elbow into it in order to relieve the pressure.

At a tradeshow I was a vendor in, there were massage therapists who were doing massage. I decided to get myself one for my shoulder.

I explained to the massage therapist what my issue

was. She listened intently, and then got to work. At first she started to work on my sore shoulder, but after about two minutes, she moved over to what I referred to as my good shoulder.

As she pressed on different parts of my good shoulder, I felt my bad shoulder burn a bit more. I reminded her of the bad shoulder. She explained to me that the shoulder that was hurting was not the problem. The real problem was the knots in my good shoulder that my bad shoulder was over compensating in. My bad shoulder was triggered by the pressure that she put on my good shoulder, and while it hurt a lot, when she was done, I felt both of my shoulders relax and loosen.

In massage therapy, trigger points are noted as sore, painful spots, also called knots that are found in the muscle. These knots are sensitive and when pressure is applied, it produces pain in a different part of the body. A trigger point massage helps to work out those knots and reduce the pain that is associated with them.

Now imagine that you treated your own triggers the same way. As little knots in your experience that are sensitive, and when pressured, they lead you to the deeper source of your pain. It may be painful in the moment, just like in the massage, and yet, the overall effects of it can be deeply healing.

Triggers can be deeply healing, as they point us in the direction of what inside of us still needs to be healed, to be loved, to be heard, and to be validated.

If we constantly walk around trying to avoid being triggered, we will only keep these wounds hidden within ourselves, while also building up more layers of protection and hurts.

When we give ourselves permission to be healed, we

also have to remember that this means the uncomfortable bits. When we say that we want to learn to do self-care; that we want to follow a spiritual path; that we want to become more self-aware; that we want to fall in love with ourselves, we need to realize that there's another side to it. By giving ourselves permission to fall in love with ourselves, we are also saying, I want to feel it all- I am willing to be triggered so I can reach a deeper level of love; I am willing to explore my inner childhood wounds so I can reach a deeper level of acceptance; I am willing to be with my Self in the darkness of my thoughts and hurts so I can reach a deeper level of truth.

It's not always easy to accept this about the healing journey.

Typically the healing journey is sold to us as a bag of crystals, a yoga retreat, a chance to connect with others who have been sold the same package, oracle card readings and messages of love and light.

No one warns you of the dark night of the soul, the destruction of everything that you once knew and believed, or that you will have to feel ALL of the feels that you have been neglecting your entire life.

I don't say this to scare you either. But rather to help you prepare to go deeper than you have ever imagined that you would.

Your triggers are your invitation to heal yourself. You get two choices. One is to get pissed off that you've been triggered, and then avoid that trigger (or person or event that created the trigger) again at all costs. The other is to note that you have been triggered, and then go and explore that a little deeper, by being with yourself and feeling the pain that is associated with it.

Depending on where you are in your own healing

journey, it may feel better to choose option one. It's not a wrong choice; sometimes we need to avoid the trigger as a part of our healing as well (so no judgment if that's what you choose).

The second option gives you an opportunity to grow beyond what your own limiting stories and beliefs have been, so that you can expand yourself beyond the story of what your experiences have been.

When you are able to see your triggers as a point of entry into a deeper aspect of who you are, you can begin to see and experience them as the gift that they are.

When you've been triggered it does feel uncomfortable. It really doesn't feel like a gift in the moment.

I have chosen both options throughout my life. There are times when I am ready to dig deep into my awareness of what is actually the problem, and times when I have run so far from the trigger because in that moment it's too painful to look at, or I have been too afraid to look deeper into it.

In my experience, the times when I have expanded beyond my own limitations were the times when I chose to step deeper into the trigger and be there with the emotions. The times when I was too afraid, or it was too painful, the same triggers kept coming back, in new and different ways.

This is the pattern of the triggers. They never really go away until we are willing to look at them, sit with them and dig deeper into ourselves. We can tuck all of our wounds away and say that we are healed, however, the trigger that is exposed will tell us differently.

I remember when I was first starting out on my healing journey, I truly believed that there was a starting point and an ending point. I thought I could look at a lot of my main experiences of hurt, heal them, and then I would be done.

I set out with stars in my eyes of how great I was going to feel when I got all of the healing work out of the way, and was able to move past my earlier experiences so that I could truly stand in the joy of the now.

What ended up happening was quite different than what I had imagined.

The more I began to be with my painful experiences, the more painful experiences would bubble up to the surface. Some for the very first time since they had happened, and some that had rolled around in my mind for decades.

A lot of times, we spend all of our time and energy focusing on 'being okay', on 'feeling happy all of the time', on 'being what we are supposed to be in order to keep everyone else comfortable'.

When we finally admit to ourselves that maybe we aren't quite as happy as we are pretending to be, and maybe we aren't okay, it's almost as though our entire body feels a huge sense of relief, and all of the memories, and emotions come bubbling up to the top, saying, 'Finally, she's ready to be with us too'.

Sometimes the trigger shows up in a conversation with a friend or family member, and sometimes the trigger is a song that brings up an old memory. Sometimes the trigger is a television show, and sometimes the trigger is what's happening in world events.

What triggers deep emotions in one person may have absolutely no effect on someone else. What one person hears in a conversation may be offensive, while another may find everything in the conversation to be a reasonable thing to say.

Our triggers are so deeply personal, and ours to own.

A few years back, we sat down as a family to watch the heavily debated TV show, 13 Reasons Why. For those who may not have watched it, it's a series that follows the story of a teenage girl who commits suicide, and leaves tapes with her classmates to explain the 13 reasons why she killed herself.

We watched with four of our children. Our oldest told us that this was not a good representation of suicide, high school or teenagers in general. She labelled the show as stupid. The two kids in the middle thought the show was boring, and lacked relatable and relevant material. Our younger daughter enjoyed it, thought it was relevant, and cried during all of the scenes meant to bring out the emotions.

For myself, I cried, from almost the first episode to the last. The experience of the young girl was very similar to my own during teenage years, and while there were different characters and outcomes, the deep hurts and vulnerable, raw emotions triggered so many of my own unhealed emotions from that time period in my life.

When it came to triggers, our teens didn't have the experience of the characters in the show, and so they weren't triggered into any of their own emotions, nor did they believe that this could actually be someone's experience.

For myself though, the show brought up a lot of emotions that I had kept buried within me for so long. After one particularly triggering episode, Jon held me as I cried, and cried. It wasn't a bad thing. I had memories surfacing of my own teenage experiences; memories that I had promptly buried and protected when I found out I was pregnant with my oldest. I was able to live for seventeen years with the pain buried, and the show triggered them to come out of the shadows and into the light.

Was it painful? Yes, absolutely. There was such a deep hurt as the shield I had kept up broke apart, and the fearful, and hurting 'little me' came out with the big emotions. There was shame that I had buried for so long that this was a part of my experience. I so badly didn't want to be seen as I was in my teenage years after I had my oldest, so I did everything I could to prevent that. And now, here I was, crying out all of these painful old stories and experiences, and exposing the hurt that I had thought I needed to carry on my own.

Was it worth it? Yes, absolutely.

By crying out the pain, by admitting to the experiences, by hearing the words coming out of my mouth for the very first time, there was a huge release. I no longer had to hide behind my experiences, or feel shameful for what they were.

Jon was able to see the pain, and hold me as I cried out the stories. He didn't try to tell me to get over it, or tell me that everything would be okay. He simply held me in the pain that I was in, soothing out the rough edges as they came piling out.

The triggers we have now are not showing up to cause more harm. They are showing up to show us all of the stuff that we have been pushing down, running away from, covering up, and pretending don't exist.

Our triggers are the light in the darkness we have been begging for; ready to illuminate all of the painful experiences so that we can step back into the truth of who we really are.

> **Heart Work**
>
> When was the last time you were triggered?
>
> Did you look deeper into it, or did you get defensive? What caused you to react the way that you did?

Chapter # 4

What's Love Got to Do with It?

The Beatles had it right when they sang out 'All you need is love', and Jason Mraz brings the truth with 'Love Is Still the Answer'.

Love is all that we have ever needed. From the moment that we were born, until the moment that we die, love is what will continue to fuel our souls and help us to reach the capacity that we are able to expand to.

Our greatest confusion comes from us looking for this love outside of ourselves. The greatest movies, songs and books of all time hold a thread of finding love with another person, who brings us back to being whole, and when that love is gone, we find ourselves broken, our hearts to never be repaired again.

More often than not, the people that we are turning to for this type of love are also broken and wounded in the same ways that we are. They have the fears, the doubts, and the unhealed experiences that they are carrying around, and so their inner children and egos are seeking that same affirmation that you are. Their own capacity to love completely openly is sheltered by the pain and the confusion they are holding inside.

But what if, instead of finding the love from another that we begin to sing these love songs to ourselves? What if instead of looking for a knight in shining armor to carry us off into the sunset, we become that knight for the child within us who is feeling broken? What if we trusted in ourselves, and our own capacity to love so much that we healed our entire being and created space for the wounded parts of ourselves to exist without judgment or criticism?

Self-love and self-care have been at the tip of every healer and life coach's tongue for the better part of the last decade. And yet, with all of the knowledge sharing that is happening on the subject, so many are getting caught up in the act of thinking a massage, a facial, or enjoying a glass of wine is an act of self-love or self-care.

And while it can be a way to show yourself love, it is still an external experience. Using external experiences as ways of promoting our own self-care regimen comes with a price, both in the literal and metaphorical sense.

When we seek something outside of ourselves to fill the void that we are feeling, we are ultimately telling ourselves that we are not enough to fill that void. That the void can only be filled through different experiences, different relationships, or different ways of giving to ourselves.

However, when we seek to fill the void with an internal acceptance, and internal love for the self, and what the story has been and experienced, we can see that we are more than enough, and more than capable of healing our own internal wounds.

Now, believe me, I definitely indulge in regular energy healing, and listening to music that I love, and going for walks in nature as ways of destressing, however, if I become dependent on these things, I start to lose out on the power of the connection that I have within myself at all times.

When I first started my healing journey (or at least became aware of it), I would hear the term self-care and self-love ALL of the time. And I got the concept of it.

I would eat my veggies, and try to drink my water. I would get an energy healing, or go see a psychic. I would listen to my favorite music, and hang out with friends. I would try to balance life at home with six kids, trying to start a business, and having a healthy relationship with my husband. But the act of 'self-love and self-care' became a point of exhaustion for me. It felt like I could never do enough or be enough to get rid of the 'burnt out feeling' that was laying just below the surface.

And so I would seek out more information on self-care, and how to practice it often. The one thing that I kept missing out on though was the ability to just be there for myself, and no one else. To just simply listen to all of the thoughts and just love them for being what they were.

I was consistently listening to others' opinions as to what my journey of self-love and self-care should look like, without actually listening to what Kevin had to say, or what would make him feel loved within my body.

By becoming the space for yourself, whether it be your ego story, or your heart's vision, at all times, you are able to break free of the societal norm that you are not enough, or that you don't have the gifts and talents to provide everything that you have ever needed. By looking outside of yourself, you are only reiterating the story that everything good comes from outside of you, from someone else's dream, from a different energy source than the one that you are.

When I first started my meditation journey, I held off for a few days because I needed to get the perfect meditation chair, and corner off an area in my bedroom to meditate in. I bought myself new journals, a new book to read in the corner, a shelf and a lamp. I was so excited by the looks of the meditation corner that I couldn't sit down to meditate when I first got it complete.

The following day, when I sat down to meditate, I realized just how impractical the corner was. It was cold.

The chair was too hard and too low to the ground. To turn the lamp on, I had to move my body to a really awkward angle.

I got up and grabbed myself some more pillows, trying to find the right way to arrange them so my neck and back and legs wouldn't be too uncomfortable.

I meditated for about five minutes before saying, screw this, and going back to my daily activities.

The following day, it was the same thing. And the day after that.

Finally, I decided to just try sitting on my couch, where I knew my comfy spot and closing my eyes. Despite the fact that my son's left over breakfast dishes were right there, and there were strewn socks on the floor, I went into a deep meditation... deeper than I ever had before.

I realized in that moment that none of the external stuff actually mattered. What mattered was my own comfortability and level of acceptance for what is, that ultimately gives me the greatest connection to myself.

And in the act of meditation, I am able to listen to the inner voice that isn't feeling so loved. I can give Kevin a space to be heard, and love him for all that he is, and all that he has experienced.

Kevin never needed a perfect meditation spot. Nor does Kevin need the right haircut, or the perfect clothes, or a massage, or lunch every Thursday with friends. And while they all feel good to have, all that Kevin ever needed was to be loved, seen, heard, and validated.

My true acts of self-love were the days when I took the time to sit and listen to what Kevin had to say, and held the space for him to have center stage, accepting everything that he had to say without trying to 'overcome it' or 'talk him out of it'. By simply being the space that he needed all along, I was able to create a loving relationship with him.

So often, our first thoughts when the fears and doubts come up is to either push them away, or latch on to what they are saying, deeming them to be true.

However, when you simply listen with a loving and open mind to what they have to say, you are showing your thoughts that they are loved just as they are. All thoughts are neither right nor wrong. They simply just are what they are.

If you have a thought that comes up that says, 'I can totally do this', and then it's followed by another thought that says, 'Oh my God, what if I can't do it', which one is right? You are the space that has both of these thoughts, and you are the space that has created both of these thoughts into existence.

The only thing that is real, is you.

Allowing yourself to have the thought without attaching yourself to the thought is the ultimate act of self-love.

Think of the thoughts that come up as being as solid as the wind. Sometimes you can feel them, sometimes you can see the way they change the environment around you. Just as the wind has the ability to be gentle and sweet, offering relief on a hot day, it also has the ability to be strong and fierce on a stormy day. It can be cold and unkind in the depths of winter, it can cause destruction in tornado or hurricane season, or it can be used to lift balloons into the air, help sailboats to cross water, and windmills to spin, producing electricity to those connected to it. Sometimes it is completely non-existence.

None of it is right or wrong. It just is what it is. And while we may complain about the weather, we also realize that the weather is not who we are.

It is the same with our thoughts and emotions. Our thoughts may be good, bad, or indifferent. We may feel very positive about the thoughts that come up, or we may feel very frightened by the things that our thoughts have to say. Regardless as to how we feel about them, they are just thoughts. They are not solidified as being the absolute truth.

And yet, many of us will have a thought, either about ourselves, or about someone or something outside of us, and grab hold of it as being the only truth that there is. We attach ourselves on to the thought and decide that it must be our ultimate truth, otherwise why would it be there?

It is in the attachment to the thought, that we become hardened in our hearts and in our thinking.

When it comes to the ego, it is through the attachment of the thoughts that the stories start to formulate that eventually fill us with fear, repressed emotion and stagnant energy. The ego in early development remembers the thoughts and feelings that came up during the experiences that we have had, and because it knows no differently, it creates those to be the truth.

We have been conditioned and shown that the only way we can live a 'spiritually-aligned-life' is to think positive, and leave those distracting emotions at the door. We have been taught to overlook our own triggers and warnings about others, and to seek out the beauty in everyone. And while these are all great things, they also bypass the very experience we are here to have..... The human experience.

The human experience can be messy. There are highs and lows, mixed in with celebration and disappointment, joy and sorry, birth and death, good and bad. The human expression for all of these are as varied as the experiences themselves, and not one of them is wrong.

Yes, that's right.
Not one of them are wrong.
Angry at your boss? Perfect!
Disappointed in your mom? Awesome!
Feeling rejected? Beautiful!
Feeling overjoyed? Wonderful!
Scared of stepping into the opportunity in front of you? Brilliant!
Every single emotion that we experience is exactly what we should be feeling in that moment.
This is the Ego showing up. This is the Ego reacting to an outer experience (or even an inner thought) that says I like this, or I don't like this, or this makes me uncomfortable. Sometimes, the Ego is giving you the emotion because of a past experience that you weren't able to express or heal, and sometimes it serves as a warning that you need to stop and head in a different direction.
Often the experiences are along the lines of 'I felt unloved, unheard, unseen or not validated in my emotions'. If the child that you once were, which has now become your ego-voice, had simply been shown that it was loved, heard, seen and validated, than the story could be rewritten. Luckily, that child is still existent within you today, and thus, the story of your past can still be rewritten, to provide you with a deeper understanding and level of self-compassion and love for who you became.
The truth is, many of us didn't know any better when we were younger. We used our best knowledge to protect, and save us from the experiences that we were having. As a result, we may have become shy, awkward, angry, fearful, untrusting, lacking in love, or feeling abandoned.

However, as adults now, we can become the parents and teachers that we wished we once had, and lead these younger aspects of ourselves out of the dark and back into the light again.

When you look at the experiences that you have had, you may be filled with guilt, shame, anger or sadness. All of those are okay. The inner child, and the ego-voice that was created during those events needs to know that they are loved, regardless of the 'why' of them being created in the first place.

This is a simple exercise that I invite you to do before moving forward throughout the rest of the book:

1. Write down the experiences that you had up until this day that you are ashamed, angry, guilty, or hurt over. These can be life changing events, or small memories that you still hold onto.
2. Beside each experience write your age, or your approximate age.
3. Ask yourself 'What feelings or stories did this experience create for me?'
4. What truth can your adult-self offer to your child-self in regards to this situation?

When I created this exercise for myself, I was able to see my own story in a brand new light. I was able to see the pain, and the hurt of the experiences, but also offer my younger selves a new sense of love and compassion for showing up in the best way that they knew how.

My Example:

At age 3, I was molested. I spent my life feeling ashamed, and angry at myself for not saying no. I took on responsibility for the pain that my molester was feeling by blaming myself for his actions. I stopped asking for help. *Today I love the 3 year old, who wanted a voice; who wanted to be safe. I give her the safety she needed then. I give her the opportunity to speak now. I listen to what she has to say.*

At age 6, I was in and out of the hospital due to illnesses. I missed over a month of school. One day, when I came back from tests, my mom and dad were not in the room. They had gone home to sleep, or to grab a coffee. I cried and cried, feeling completely alone in the world. *Today I love the 6 year old, who was feeling alone in the hospital; who just wanted her mom and dad; who was tired of the tests; and cried while drawing pictures in art. I let her know she is not alone now. I let her rest. I give her the comfort she needs when she just can't take it anymore.*

At age 8, I have a faint memory of another sexual assault. I remember the 'before'. I remember the 'after'. I don't know what happened in between, or if I can even say it was a sexual assault. I have been angry at myself for not remembering, for not having the details, for not keeping myself safe again. *Today I love the 8 year old, who seems to have forgotten. It hurts too much to look at. I tell her that is okay with me. I help her find the good memories, we can focus on that for now.*

At age 10, I broke a window in the barn/tool shed, when I hit a baseball right through it. I wasn't in trouble, but I sure felt guilty. It was replaced the next day. The following day while leaving the barn, the wind caught hold of the door that the window was in, and the window smashed again. The guilt and shame were exemplified. *Today I love the 10 year old, who felt guilt and shame for breaking the window, not once but twice. I assure her we all make mistakes and she is perfect just as she is.*

At age 13, I was bullied. I was too fat, too smart, too loud, too much for everyone. I tried to lose weight, I tried to dumb it down, and I tried to stay quiet. I started to seek a deeper spiritual truth. I was ashamed of who I was, I was angry for not being 'cool enough' to stand out, and not 'cool enough' to simply disappear. I felt alone and awkward. *Today I love the 13 year old, who hated her body, the inauthenticity of school and started to seek out a deeper meaning in life. I tell her it was through her loneliness that I am able to be who I am today. I thank her for wanting to learn more. I thank her for giving me permission to tell my story. I thank her for seeking out answers in a world that didn't make sense.*

At age 17, I tried to commit suicide more than once. I was grieving the loss of my father, the loss of my family, and the loss of a baby. I was angry and bitter at life. I hated everyone, and mainly myself. I turned the self-loathing into cigarettes, sex, alcohol and missing school. *Today I love the 17 year old, the one ready to give up on life. I let her know she was strong, but that the weakness she felt is loved as well. I tell her she gives me strength today when I want to give up. She got through all of that. Surely I can get through my stresses now. She carries the grief, and anger and bitterness. I tell her that is okay. Today I will carry her.*

At age 24, I left a marriage, and began to seek out a deeper meaning in life. I was embarrassed to have been this 'bright person' when I was younger, only to become a single mom of 3 before I was 25. I was ashamed of my lack of depth in society, working as a waitress. I was still carrying that anger from all of those years of building it up, and I was ready to get a fresh start on life, regardless of the effort that it would take. *Today I love the 24 year old, lost and broken, thinking surely there is more to life than this. I let her be lost in my body. I accept her as she is. I show her the magic that has been created in her confusion. I thank her for wanting more, for wanting a deeper sense of purpose, for wanting to make an impact.*

As you can see in the example, I had been enough the entire time, just as you have always been enough. It was through my experiences that I began to think that I was not, and allowed Kevin to start to take over. As each story grew on to the other one, the anger, the fears, the feelings of being abandoned and alone only grew. This was what Kevin knew, and this was how Kevin reacted to every experience.
Anger. Guilt. Shame. Embarrassment. Fear. Self-Loathing. Self-Hatred.
In looking at the messages in bold/italics I am able to see what Kevin has been looking for this entire time:

Kevin needs to feel safe. Kevin needs his voice to be heard, in all circumstances. Kevin needs to know he is not alone, and to feel comforted when he is feeling as though he is alone. Kevin needs to remember the good memories, as much, if not more so than the bad memories. Kevin needs to forgive himself for the mistakes he has made. Kevin likes to learn, and to understand deeper concepts in life. In that, Kevin feels he has more to offer, and more to understand in humanity, which helps him to feel better when humanity isn't being so kind. Kevin started to write as a way of expressing the voice that needed to be heard. Kevin has been the strength that has carried this lifetime through.

Seeing Kevin in this new light, I realized that he was nothing to be ashamed or embarrassed by. He was nothing to be hidden away, or act as though he didn't exist in the first place.

It was actually through the pain and hurt of what 'we' had experienced together that I was able to create a blue print for everything that my Soul was wanting to become in this lifetime.

Without the painful experiences, I would not be writing this book now. Without the strong ego attachment to the old stories, and the heart's desire to dig for a deeper truth, I wouldn't be writing this book now. Every single piece of who I was, every single hurt that Kevin carried, were all leading up until this moment. Here. Right now. And this is the perfection of it all.

Rather than shaming myself and ego for existing in the first place, I began to look at it all through the lens of love, allowing myself to see the character(s) that were created through the experiences, and rather than claiming them to be the absolute truth, I gently showed them a more loving way to look at themselves and their experience.

It was through these new acts of love that I became the knight in shining armor that Kevin needed. It was through these acts of love, that I started to sing the greatest love songs to myself. It was through these new acts of love that I was able to heal and hear the inner versions of my younger self, and carry them through the inner storms of hurt to a place of love and peace.

Heart Work

Do the exercise in this chapter.

1. Write down the experiences that you had up until this day that you are ashamed, angry, guilty, or hurt over. These can be life changing events, or small memories that you still hold onto.
2. Beside each experience write your age, or your approximate age.
3. Ask yourself 'What feelings or stories did this experience create for me?'
4. What truth can your adult-self offer to your child-self in regards to this situation?

\

Chapter #5

Do You Hear What I Hear?

Working with the Ego in this new way allows you to begin an inner dialogue that is not based on just the facts that your Ego is pointing out to you, but rather, opens you to a new way of viewing the dialogue that is happening with you.
Most of us suffer from monkey brain.
In any given moment, we can be thinking of many different things at once, from grocery lists, things we need to accomplish, worries of what happened yesterday, and anxiety about what tomorrow will bring. We can be conscious of these thoughts, however, more often than not, they are running in the background, like a constant white noise that we have no control over.
When we are not paying attention to the thoughts and inner dialogue that we are having, it can become like a monster that is distorting the reality around us.
The inner dialogue presents a new challenge for us, as it creates new scenarios, based on past events, to tell us what the information that we are receiving 'must mean'.
Anyone who has had a conversation that left them feeling uncomfortable knows exactly what I am talking about.
You go out for lunch with a friend. You are having a great time.
At one point, she tells you that you wouldn't understand what she's talking about, as your relationship is always perfect.
Your relationship isn't perfect though. You and your

partner had a fight last night. If your friend had stopped talking long enough, you would have been able to tell her. But now you can't. She will think you're trying to hoard the attention. So you stay quiet.

All the way home from lunch, you feel more and more angry. How dare she point out your perfect relationship? Is your relationship perfect and you're too selfish to see it? Are you just ungrateful? Are you a bad listener? Is that why she said you wouldn't understand? Are you a bad friend? Does she even like you?

Does anyone even like you? Probably not. You're such a loser. Even your partner doesn't like you. Or at least that's how it seems. No one has ever really liked you, or understood you or where you are coming from.

Everyone thinks life is always just perfect.

No one can see the truth.

I don't want them to see the truth anyways, they would probably hate me even more.

Why do I even bother?

While this is just an example, it is the way most of our brains function with anything that leaves us feeling uncomfortable. We feel the uncomfortable feeling, which in this case is anger, resentment, rejection and hurt. And then the thoughts start to filter in, filling our mind with questions, and taking it from an uncomfortable feeling to an all-out inner self-loathing experience.

An unloved and unseen ego starts to fill in the answers to the questions, often adding aggravation and hurt to the experience.

The greatest question you can ask yourself when this starts to happen is: **Is this the Truth? Or is this the trigger?**

Because the Ego is a culmination of all of our

experiences up until this point, the ego only knows the level of truth from the past. This level of truth from the past is based on old operating systems, and expired stories from when we were one, or five or nine. All of the painful experiences and memories that you looked at in the last chapter, are the basis for what your Ego believes to be true, but what your Soul is able to see as simply being a trigger.

The Ego identifies with the trigger. The Ego identifies with the pain, and hurt that it has experienced in the past, and uses that information to form an idea of what the truth in the new situation is. When the trigger happens, the Ego has an opportunity to be seen... in its anger, frustration, sadness, and fear.

And in that opportunity to be seen, it often reacts, based on the pains of the past. This is not done to hurt you, but rather to 'save you' from being hurt, like you have been in the past. However, because it's based on the past, quite often the way it shows up is similar to a child having a temper tantrum or melt down; not something any adult wants to publicly display.

When the Ego has been triggered, you may feel as though you have no control over what you are saying, doing or the ways that you are behaving. With the Ego in complete control, you may find yourself regretting your choices after the initial trigger has passed.

When you are able to start identifying the parts of your Ego, and what your triggers are, you can begin to expand yourself beyond what the triggers are, and see the truth in the situation. The truth comes from a level that is beyond the Ego, and the Ego's creation. The truth comes from a deep place within you: your heart, your Soul, God; you get to choose what you want to call it.

It is in that deep place within you that you can begin to step away from the attachments to what the story has been, and allow yourself to become a witness to the story and the ways that the story is making itself shown to you now.

One of my own big triggers is reacting in anger when I feel as though someone is lying to me, or taking something of mine. I demand honesty in all situations, and will call someone out on their bullshit if I feel it necessary.

This isn't the worst habit to have (my built-in lie detector works amazingly well) however, when someone would lie to me, or steal from me, I would become quite irate. Often displaying extreme anger, with my entire body shaking, and finally melting through a fit of tears. I only wanted the truth. Even if the truth hurt.

Through working with my Ego, Kevin started to show me the ways in which I was lied to as a younger child, being told that everything was okay, when everything was not. I was able to see the ways that my inner child had felt as though the innocence was stolen through the molestation.

My anger at liars and thieves was more so about what my own experiences had been than what it was about the people who were lying and stealing from me.

On the human level, I am able to see that lying and stealing are both morally wrong. I am able to determine that my conscious chooses to be morally 'correct'.

On a Soul level, I had to dig deeper and become a greater space for the trigger to just simply be there. Rather than trying to fix it, or react in anger, or crying it out, I had to just let it be.

Sitting with the trigger was not fun. It never is. It is sitting with an uncomfortable emotion and not allowing yourself to leave until you find peace at the end of the tunnel. Sometimes it feels like you're suffocating, sometimes it feels as though there are a thousand other things that your Ego is wanting you to occupy yourself with. It may feel like heaviness on the chest, boredom to get it done, or anger that you need to sit there in the first place (like a child on a time out!)

I believe I displayed all of these examples when I sat down to be with this trigger. Kevin showed up at his finest. He was angry, he was hurt, and he wanted to prove others wrong. Most importantly, others lying felt unsafe... very unsafe to Kevin and what Kevin's experiences had been.

My job here wasn't to make Kevin go away just because he was showing up loudly. My job here wasn't to find a solution to the problem we were having in the experience. My job here wasn't to change Kevin's point of view, or anyone else's behavior... not even my own.

My only job was to listen.

To listen to the fears that were coming up, to listen to the anger, to listen to the hundreds of voices and thoughts that were coming up.

The voice that said this is bullshit.

The voice that said I'm so tired of this.

The voice that said I'm about to have a heart attack.

The voice that said I can't trust anyone.

The voice that asked what did I do to deserve this.

The voice the asked what makes me so unsafe that others need to lie to me?

The voice that wondered if this was just another life lesson.

The voice that demanded that life on earth is just bull, and from now on I would only be a Spirit Guide. No more human-ness for me.

The voice that was afraid to speak up at all.

Oh, I could go on and on. The Ego has many voices,

many faces, many fears and many hurts.

And as I sat there, I was able to witness them all. I couldn't change the pain, or answer the questions, or assure no more life on Earth, but I could listen.

And so I did.

I listened and listened and listened some more. My body went from feeling panicky, and angry, to feeling peace and contentment.

By listening to the trigger, and not reacting as I had in the past, but rather sitting with the trigger and listening to what my entire being needed to say, I was able to become the safety that I needed so many times.

By witnessing the pain, rather than morphing into the pain, I was able to let it be there, to be seen in its full light, and just love it.

And it was in that, that the pain and the fear and the anger and the anxiety all started to leave.

My life was not in jeopardy based on another's actions. My life was perfectly safe. My Ego though, based on its own experiences of feeling unsafe in the energy of someone lying or stealing wasn't able to see that. And thus, the experiences were triggering an old story. The truth was that I was safe. The truth was that I was not in danger. The truth was that I could be the space for the trigger to be present, and to love it, and in that, it would start to melt away on its own.

The deep place inside knows this truth, but so often we are caught up in the mind's point of view of what the experience is, that we are unable to reach the truth. It's only in the silence of the world around us that we are able to dig deeper into this place of truth, and hold ourselves so lovingly to allow the healing to occur.

Simon and Garfunkel had it right when they sang of the Sound of Silence.

Hello darkness, my old friend, I've come to talk with you again.

So often in these busy and hectic times we call life, we are so distracted… by television, music, social media, gossip magazines, and a constant 'connection' to the world. More often than not, we don't have a chance to disconnect from the world, and 'connect within'.

When we give ourselves the space to step back into the darkness, as though it's an old friend just wanting to catch up, and reconnect, we give ourselves the space to start healing… not just in our minds, but in our entire being.

The dark bits of who we are, the parts that cause us to feel the anger, the frustration, and the hurt (basically all of those uncomfortable feelings) is the connection that we have been looking for all along.

It is through the darkness, and listening to what it has to say, that we are able to reveal a deeper truth to ourselves. It's not always easy, but it's always worth it.

> **Heart Work:**
>
> Sit in silence. You can start with small intervals if you like, however, try for longer spaces of time. Listen to what your Ego is showing you, and allow yourself to be the witness. Take note of the shifts happening within your body. Allow yourself to feel the deeper truths that are revealed to you. Every day try to extend the time you are sitting with the silence for deeper truths to be revealed to you.

Chapter # 6

Validation

The more you sit within the silence and allow yourself to bear witness to what it is your Ego is showing you, the more validated the Ego begins to feel, and the less dominating it becomes in your life.

This may sound counterintuitive to some, however, the more attention you are able to give to the ego and validate the experience that it has lived, the quieter the Ego becomes. It is no longer fighting for attention, but rather, is receiving the attention that it desired in the first place, from you.

It is much like working with a child. A child who is feeling unloved, unheard, unsafe and invalidated in their experience is more likely to act out in order to get attention, even if it's negative attention. Some is better than none after all.

As the parent to the Ego, it is your duty to create a loving space that is able to validate what the ego's experience has been, even when it's not the truth (or how you have been able to view it from your older perspective.)

The adult-self is quick to come in with a mature perspective of what happened in the experience, and as such, tends to dismiss the emotions that the child-self (ego) experienced in the first place.

A while back, my husband was talking about his own childhood experiences and I had encouraged him to work on the exercise that I have shown you in chapter 3. From my outside perspective, I could see that a very painful experience for him happened when he was six, and learned that his cousin, and classmate was killed in a car accident. Death can be a very scary thing for many adults, and hard to comprehend for children. In the result of his cousin's death, my husband was not able to attend the funeral (because back then it was frowned upon).

His adult-self went straight into explaining to me how it wasn't that big of a deal. They weren't as close as they could have been. It was a shock. But it wasn't a big thing. He was mad that he didn't get to go to the funeral, but that was the way things were. Death was a secret. There was a lot of whispers. He was using the story of his cousin's death as a crutch.

The excuses he came up with were far and wide, and everything in between.

I stopped him and asked him how our son, who is 7, would react if he found out his cousin or a classmate had passed.

Our son is very open emotionally, and takes everything to heart... from the death of a worm on the sidewalk spending too much time in the sun, to the starving children around the world... he is always wanting to make a world of peace and love and happiness.

To see him in the state of losing someone, we both know that he would be heartbroken. He would cry. He would wonder why and how. He would want answers. He would want to be held. He would want to know that he was safe and that it was okay to be sad.

By removing himself from the situation and putting our son in the perspective of a young child, my husband was able to see just how devastating it would be for any child to lose someone, regardless of the closeness.

In that, he was able to start to hold the space for the younger part of him that had a lot of questions and needed the reassurance that he was okay.

So often we disregard our experiences as being 'not a big deal' however, when you are a child, or when you are in the middle of experiencing something, it IS a big deal!

Our ideals of being 'strong', of 'pushing through' and 'moving forward' are all great and everything, however, an important step in that is recognizing and validating just how fucking hard it can be at times.

At the end of the day, it is the Ego that is experiencing it all in the gruesome human experience, and the Soul is witnessing it all, knowing that something deeper and more magical is at play. But when you're operating from the Ego (and are completely unaware of it) you are also completely unaware of the Soul that is watching and holding the space.

When we allow ourselves to validate the experience that we have had, we give the Ego a chance to be seen, heard and loved. So often, we are running completely from the Ego's experience that we are unable to see that it's even there in the first place. Add on top of it the negative vibes that Ego has received from the new age and self-help community, and the Ego is suddenly shunned into the corner so we can reach our spiritual abyss.

Yes, to our adult selves the Ego's experience may seem small and petty, it may feel like it's not a very big deal at all, and yet, if your body and mind are still being triggered into the same emotions that the experience brought up for you in the first place, chances are it's actually a bigger deal than what you originally thought it to be.

When my daughter was 10, I went to see a friend, Christine, for an Emotional Code session. The idea of the session was to ask three questions on different areas that were bothering you, and then she would use muscle testing to see what emotions were being held in your body, and at what age those emotions became most dominant.

Two of my emotions that came up for me were around guilt and shame. Now if I were to look at my life and the times that I felt guilt and shame, I would look at when I was a toddler and molested, a child and stole a penny candy from the corner store, or snuck a cookie when I was supposed to be in bed asleep. I would look at my teenage years and the shame that came up around discovering my sexual drive. I would look at my early pregnancy, my early marriage, my even earlier divorce. There were many things that my adult mind could comprehend as being something that I should be ashamed and feeling guilty with.

However, what came up in the session was that it had to do with an experience that I had when I was ten years old.

I searched and searched my mind. There was nothing significant that came up for me. Christine continued with her work, I cried some, and left feeling better. My mind though was still questioning what the heck happened when I was ten that would be presenting these problems that now seemed like such a big deal.

As I drove home, a memory came to mind. My sister and I were playing baseball in our back yard. We shared a duplex-type house with our grandparents, where we lived on one side, and our grandparents lived on the other. There was a door on the inside that allowed you to step into each other's houses whenever we needed to talk.

On this particular day of playing baseball, I hit the ball hard, and it went flying…. Right into the window on the door of the barn-shed that stood at the back of the property. I was panicked. I had to tell my grandparents that I broke their window.

Rather than using the inside door, I went around to

their garage, stepped inside and rang the doorbell. I wanted to make this as formal as possible.

I told them everything. They smiled at me, and told me that it was okay. Accidents happen after all. They would get the window replaced. No harm, no foul.

The day after the window got replaced, my sister and I were upstairs in the barn, which we had converted into our clubhouse, complete with books, art supplies, and an old record player.

Getting hungry, we decided to leave. It was a windy day, and when I opened the barn door, the wind caught hold of it, slamming it up against the side of the barn. To my total dismay, the brand new window shattered in the wind's force.

I can still feel the panic in my chest, even as I type this. I thought for sure I would be grounded for a year, or punished in some other horrific way.

Again, I went into my grandparent's garage, and paced back and forth for about 30 minutes (although it felt like a lot longer) before I gathered the strength and courage to let them know just what the heck was up.

Again, I rang the doorbell, and explained, more nervously this time, just what had happened.

Again, they smiled, and told me that accidents happen. This time though, I would need to help my grandfather in the garden picking potatoes in order to pay off my debt.

It was really not a terrifying experience, however, the memory had risen up from the depths of my body, so it must have meant something.

When my daughter came home from school that day, she asked if she could go back over to the school on her bike to ride around the property. I allowed her to go, but less than 10 minutes later she returned, in absolute tears. Her brake line had popped off on the bike, and she had ridden into the school, breaking one of the windows.

To me, it was a total confirmation that my own window breaking history had been the cause of the guilt and shame that were released from my body earlier that day, and it gave me the perfect opportunity to speak to my daughter, with the same love and kindness that my grandparents had with me.

I validated her by expressing how much I understood the fear, and shame that she was feeling. I told her that I knew that she hadn't meant to do it, and we all make mistakes.

It was in that moment that I was able to see myself at her exact age, and the panic, shame and fear that came with it. This was what I had been holding onto, and because my adult-self had dismissed it as being 'not a big deal', I almost lost the opportunity to heal it in a much bigger way.

Many of us look at our triggers and our traumas as needing to be this really big thing. And believe me, sometimes they are. But sometimes, the emotional response of the body is due to smaller experiences, where you felt such a big emotion, in such a small act or experience that you end up dismissing it as not being valid at all.

When it comes to healing yourself or other people, there is no such thing as an invalid emotional response. All of your feelings, all of your emotions that are tied to an experience are absolutely perfect for you.

This doesn't mean that you need to hold onto them though.

You can be the space that you were needing when you were younger than what you are now. The 'child experiences' do not have to be 'the times before you were eighteen and legally considered to be an adult'. The 'child experiences' are anything that has happened before this moment now. Who you were at the beginning of starting this book, or starting this day, is no longer the same as who you are now.

We are all constantly growing and learning, and shedding off the layers of our pasts as we step more so into the truth of who we are.

In that, it's so important that we hold the space for ourselves and validate ourselves for the experience that we have had. Most often we apologize for feeling the way that we have felt, or we dismiss it as not being a big deal, or that we are overreacting, or underreacting, or....

The truth is, the list could go on and on with all of the bullshit stories that we tell ourselves about how we should be feeling, rather than simply accepting how we are actually feeling in the moment.

It is in our resistance to what these emotions are that they begin to grow bigger and bigger, and feel more and more uncomfortable. If we pause to acknowledge the emotions that are coming up and validating what we are experiencing, the emotions then have the opportunity to be seen, to be heard, to be validated, and to move on.

One of my greatest triggers in my adult years has been people who lie to me. When a lie is told around me, it's as though a panic button goes off in my chest. My heart thuds louder, my ears grow hotter. I literally feel the blood boiling under my skin. I want to scream, 'Liar! Liar!'

This has come forward in the simplest of lies (a person saying they will do one thing and then doing another) or in bigger lies (a person stealing from me and then directly lying to me, telling me that I am the reason the stealing has happened).

Whether it's a big lie, or a small lie, in my body it

feels the same. Whether it was a big lie, or a small lie, I was reacting.

Realizing that there was a trigger in regards to people lying, I decided to dig deeper. I could see that the core of my trigger stemmed back to my early childhood when I was molested. The lie that was told around that was that I would be safe around him, that I needed to trust him that I needed to respect him.

However, in my teenage years, I had also been a liar, and a thief, often stealing clothes from my sister, or small items from stores in our neighborhood.

In later teenage years, and early adulthood, boyfriends cheated on me, friends betrayed me.

And I had done the same to others.

So was this such a sore spot for me because others had been doing it to me for my entire life? Or was it because I also had done it to others throughout my life?

It would be easiest for me to blame this on all of the 'others' in my life. However, I knew in that, the only common denominator was.... Myself.

I started focusing my meditations on revealing to myself how to shift the energy around this trigger. One part of my mind wanted to blame others, one part of my mind wanted to blame myself, one part thought we should just forgive it all, and one part said fuck it, people need to stop their lying. The problem with my mind was not that it was so chatty, but that it had so many differing points of view, and all of them were valid. But if I truly wanted to shift this, I needed to reach the level of my heart, the part of my soul that was connected with the entire Universe that had already experienced it all, and knew something beyond my limited ego-stories of what this was and what it should look like.

As I listened to the many voices of my ego, my heart

started to take a deeper perspective of all of the triggers.

First off, the validation that my ego was looking for was simple. My ego had felt unsafe, and used the alarm bells when liars and thieves to warn me that I had to get the hell out of dodge if I wanted to divert another disaster.

But the bigger part of my heart, the one that was connected not to the limited story, but rather the vastness of the Universe, was able to start showing me all of the times that I had been met with liars, and was able to rise above and walk away, setting clear boundaries for myself and greater intentions for the roads ahead.

If it was possible for me to feel the energy of a liar, and I had the means necessary to walk away or set clearer boundaries as I had shown in the past, then I was actually completely safe right where I was. I didn't need to defend anything, or react with anger, or feel completely small and burdened by their untruths.

The other piece of validation that my ego was looking for was forgiveness for myself for all of my past mistakes. And in true human fashion, I had made many, and resented myself for almost as much. These lies and the stealing that I had done in my past were a deep part of my shadows, and as much as I stepped into being a 'good person' in my adult years, the energy of what I had done in my past remained lurking in the shadows, just waiting for someone to bring it up and make me look like a fraud.

And so I sat with my heart longer, willing these shadow aspects out of the closet even more, to reveal themselves to me fully.

Instead of being met with shame, or even anger, I was met with an immense sadness and a need and desire to control everything that was going wrong in my life. I hadn't been a bad person, I had simply been a confused one, a lost

Soul, just trying to make myself feel better for just a moment. Of course, material things and breaking connections with others through lying never truly helps you to 'feel better' but desperate times call for desperate measures.

Rather than pushing these shadows back into the closet, I saw them for what they were. These shadows were a lot of what had created the personality traits of Kevin, the greatest part of my ego. The fears, the abandonment, the rejections. Scolding this inner part of me would no longer work. It hadn't worked in the past, for my parents, my teachers or myself.

I needed to show love, compassion and validation for everything that Kevin /I had experienced when these shadows were becoming the most dominant force.

And so the validation process began; with two hands on my heart, still sitting in the meditation, and simply reminding myself that I was loved and cherished, even with everything else that I had done. I was no longer holding this as a bomb threat over my head. I was ready to let this go.

Me: *I love you*

Ego: *But why? I'm such a fucking disaster!*

Me: *You are beautiful. You are perfect, right where you are. I know you're hurting. I know you feel unsafe. I love you in that. I hold you in that. You can feel that way with me.* I feel the energy in my hands getting hotter, as I whisper these words to the broken pieces of me.

Ego: *But I just keep fucking up. I can't get anything right! I am worthless.*

Me: *You can feel that way. I will love you while you feel that. All of you is safe with me.*

Ego: *Everyone should hate me. I hate me.*

Me: *That's okay. Hate yourself. I will love you while you hate yourself.*

Ego: *Wait. What?*

Me: *Whatever you need to feel. Whatever makes you feel validated for where you're at right now…? I will love you. I do love you. I am loving you. Right here. Right now. You are safe.*

Ego: (Tears. Crying. Chills running through the body. A complete sense of relief).

Ego: *But I have messed up. I have made mistakes. I have been mean. I have been ruthless. I have been selfish.*

Me: *You have been exactly who you needed to be at the time. And I love you for that. You felt hurt… and you reacted to that hurt by making the choices that you made, and I love you for that. You were defending yourself, and I love you for that. You were afraid of being hurt, and so you pushed others away, and I love you for that. You have sought out ways to take away your pain, and I am so grateful for that. I can love you for all of the small ways that you have been feeling. I can love you for all of the things that you have done. I can hold you while you feel ashamed. You are safe with me.*

And so it went, this conversation between myself and my Ego. The Ego kept creating more reasons as to why I shouldn't love it, and my heart stated, I'm going to love you anyway.

We continued like this for a few weeks, and as we did, the tightness in my chest, the heaviness on my shoulders started to melt away.

I began to notice a trigger, rather than reacting to it, bringing a deeper awareness to myself that I was being triggered, and my defenses were starting to come up. Rather than stepping into the trigger, I was able to witness the feelings and sensations in my body and start a conversation from that point, rather than diving deep back into the old pain and recapturing all of its initial reactions.

By validating everything that the Ego had been sharing with me, and loving it anyway, the Ego started to flow easier, to not demand as much attention, to not crave a right or a wrong to every situation.

I went from defending myself, to allowing all perspectives to be a part of my reality. In validating my Ego, I no longer needed the validation of others, nor was I triggered when I was feeling invalidated.

This became highlighted to me when one of our children was caught stealing from my husband's wallet. This was a part of my step-son's pattern, his own defense mechanism for whatever was going on in his own mind. He would steal, and then create chaos around him, so that we as parents were feeling as though it was somehow our fault that he was creating the choices that he was making.

On this particular day, I found him with his hand in his dad's wallet, looking for money. My husband doesn't take his wallet with him anywhere, and that morning had asked me for money to take along with him to work. I handed him the cash. When I caught him, I simply stated, 'That is not your wallet, and you don't have permission to go through it'.

'Dad told me I could take money from his wallet for school today', he told me.

The trigger started in my body. This was a lie. My husband and I have great communication skills, especially in regards to things revolving the children.

'Your dad had no money in his wallet today. He asked me for some before he left for work. Please put the wallet back where you found it. You don't have permission to go through it' I replied.

'This house is fucking bullshit!' he yelled, slamming the wallet down on the shelf. 'I fucking hate it here! I can't even go in my own dad's wallet? This is bullshit'.

With that, he turned and stomped out the front door, slamming it loudly behind him.

My body was shaking. Teenagers were hard, but with him, it always seemed to be much harder, the chaotic energies perpetuating our house every time he didn't get his own way or was caught doing something that he shouldn't be.

Normally, my reaction would be to feel the anger, to cry, to have my body shake for hours later. Living with him at times was like living with an abusive, explosive partner.

However this time, I placed my hands on my heart and whispered:

It's okay for you to feel angry. It's okay for you to feel unsafe. You have every right to be pissed off. Your feelings are safe with me.

I repeated this a few times, for no more than 30 seconds. The more I repeated it, the calmer I began to feel.

What typically would have me feeling down all day,

left my entire being in less than a minute.

By validating what my experience was in that moment, and the feelings that were attached to it, I didn't have to sit in resistance to the emotions all day.

So often, we resist how our bodies are feeling. We replay an experience over and over again, trying to justify our reactions, our experiences and our emotions. But this just keeps the story playing on and on. At times we may even question the truth of events, adding a white lie here or there, to be able to verify our story or version of truth as being the right one.

And it's all done in a way to distract ourselves from what it is we are truly feeling. A part of us is wanting to resist the emotions because they are uncomfortable, however, when you give yourself the permission to feel as you are feeling and the validation that it's totally normal for you to feel this way under the circumstances, the emotions don't hold on so much.

As Peter McWilliams said, Emotion is Energy in Motion.

Nothing about emotions is stagnant, or stuck, or solidified. It all has the ability to brush past us. It is only in our resistance to it, that we grab hold of them, and hold onto them for longer than we should.

A year ago, I took a trip to Monterey, California for a 6 day meditation retreat. Before the retreat even began, I sat on the beach, watching the most magnificent waves I had ever seen.

I could see the waves building in the distance, the force of them growing larger and larger, until they reached the massive rocks darting out of the shore, or the shore itself where they would simply disappear.

As I sat there, I realized that these waves that the

ocean was producing were very much like the emotions that we all feel so intensely. The rumble of them starts from somewhere deep within, and gather speed and energy as they boil to the surface.

We can choose to be like the rocks, holding on so solidly to our opinions, our beliefs, our judgements, and have the emotions crash down on us hard.

Or we can move in the flow of the emotions, allowing them to come up, and then release, just like the sands on the shoreline.

The choice is totally up to us.

Over the six days, I continuously walked down to the beach to watch the waves. While I had been to an ocean in the past, I had never been so captivated by the force and essence that these waves were bringing forward.

On the 5th day, we were given instructions to leave the retreat, and stay in silence until the next morning. For someone who likes to chatter away, this was a difficult feat. I hadn't realized before just how much I used small talk to distract the emotions that were hiding below the surface.

I made my way back down to the beach in silence, and sat down. The waves were the largest I had ever seen in my life. *How fitting,* I thought, as I sat there, my own waves of emotions coming up, over and over again.

The more I watched the growing strength of the waves, the more I felt the waves of emotions surfacing in my body. I hadn't realized just how much I had been storing inside of myself. I felt everything: frustration, anger, sadness, shame, guilt, fear.

But rather than running from them, or standing as firm as the rocks in front of me, I sat there and became more like the shore: witnessing the incoming wave, knowing that it would hit, and allowing it to shift me in whatever way I needed to be shifted, so that it could truly roll off of me.

I had heard so many times, 'Just go with the flow', however, until that moment, I had never truly felt the power that came in the non-effort of just going with the flow.

As wave after wave of emotion came up, I let the tears fall, and held the vision of the waves, knowing that as tumultuous as they looked, they would subside.

I didn't need to understand where these emotions were coming from. I didn't need to identify an experience that I was holding onto. I simply needed to be still, and allow them to come up, validating that they were real, and that I was ready to feel them.

In that, my energy began to shift. In that, I began to look at myself not as someone with strength, or who was broken, but rather just the 'I' that I am.

I was not the emotions that I had held onto for so long, but rather, just the space that held onto the emotions thinking that I needed to grasp them and understand them in order to truly heal.

All I needed was self-validation that I was loved and whole and complete, with or without all of the emotions. I simply just learned how to love myself.

Heart Work:

Part 1

Grab your journal or some paper. Jot down your triggers… what makes you the angriest? What makes you feel unsafe? What experiences have you had that knocked you out of your own spiritual alignment?

Looking at these triggers, what is the common theme that comes up for them? What emotion do you experience from them?

Looking even further, in what ways in your life, have you created the exact same or similar experience for people around you? What kind of emotions were you experiencing at the time that turned you to behave in this manner?

Part 2

Sit in silence, or with meditation music playing in the background. Thinking of the triggers that we talked about in Part 1 of this Heart Work Exercise, allow yourself to connect with your Ego and have a conversation.

What is your Ego's side of the story?

How does your heart respond?

This may take more than one try in order for you to hear and understand what your heart is showing you. As you sit there, put your hands on your heart, and offer yourself Love for whatever emotions that the triggers bring up.

Repeat. Repeat. Repeat.

Chapter # 7

The Untruths of Thoughts

The more you begin to work with your Ego, the more you will begin to understand the untruths of your own thoughts. Now, for some, this may be a hard pill to swallow. How can we be thinking of something that isn't true, especially when it feels so true for us?

Just because we think it, doesn't make it true.

Our thoughts, just like emotions, are simply passing through. When we grab hold of a thought as being the absolute truth, we limit ourselves from experiencing all aspects of life.

When we are at a space in our lives where we are able to recognize that it is simply a thought that we are having, and we have an awareness that we are not the thought but rather the creator of the thought, we can begin to shift how much we are willing to hold onto it, and how much we are ready to let go.

To bring awareness to your thoughts, simply just listen. As you're reading this book, you may notice yourself having flashbacks to earlier childhood experiences, and your thoughts ranting on that. You may notice yourself wanting to put the book down to go and do the dishes, or watch the show, or spend time with your partner. You may notice yourself saying this is stupid, or you may notice yourself agreeing with what I'm writing.

And all of these thoughts could be happening ALL at the same time.

By listening to the running commentary that is

playing in your mind, you will start to recognize just how busy the mind can become, and just how many untruths there truly are existing in your mind.

Taking a moment now to notice what's in my thoughts as I am writing this book, I can hear my thoughts say:

- Don't tell them about your thoughts. That's stupid. No one cares. Get back to writing
- Stop dragging this out.
- You have to pick your son up in 2 hours, get back to work.
- It's so nice out today
- I should probably be walking rather than sitting here to write
- How would I get the book done though?
- I still have to reply back to that email
- I need another coffee
- The rest of the house must be so neglected right now since I'm focusing on writing my book
- They would probably just ignore me anyway
- Just like I'm ignoring them
- Oh, a butterfly
- I guess I'm transforming
- Not transforming much since there's still so many thoughts happening
- I need to stretch
- I hope this isn't too personal
- I hope it's personal
- What are they thinking as they read this I wonder?
- Would they even let me know?
- Do I even want to know?

I'm sure you get the idea.

I am only one person, and yet, I am completely capable of having an entire conversation in my head, with varying points of view, varying degrees of trust and fear, anger and rebellion, peace and love, all at the same freaking time.

So what thought is true? What question should I let my mind follow?

And the answer is none of them.

As I sat here and listened to my thoughts I am aware of all of the different parts of me that are stepping out. There's the part of me that's afraid of rejection. The part of me that feels she needs to prove something, to be something for everyone. The part of me that sees the beauty of a butterfly; and the part of me that feels worthless if I'm not there for everyone else. Part of me wants to distract me from writing, while a part of me wants to sit and write forever.

I was able to recognize all of them for what they were, and rather than agreeing with them and walking away from the computer, or following the lead down a rabbit hole of self-hate, I listened to them for what they were, and validated each of them as they came up.

It is in these moments, when the thoughts are running rampant, that we are able to tap into our true innate power. Where we can be the observer of our lives, rather than the willing and compliant puppet to whatever the mind schemes up.

The more you are working with your Ego, the more you will begin to notice the separation of you and your thoughts. And in that separation, you will begin to see that you are not the thoughts themselves, but rather the space that has created them. Like a mother with her children, we can view the children, and see parts of ourselves in them, however, we are not our children. Yes, we partook in creating them, but they are an entity all on their own, with their own personalities, their own beliefs, their own desires and their own fears.

When you can treat your thoughts (and all of the parts of your Ego that come up as your thinking them) as though they are all children, fighting for attention, longing to be seen, heard and loved, AND at the same time, realize that none of them are actually you, than your thoughts will become simply 'distractions' from the truth of who you are.

Our painful thoughts can easily distract us from our truth, and our truest nature.

It is similar to when we get a toothache, or a hangnail. We may go through our entire life not connecting to the sensation of one part of our tooth, or finger, and yet, when something is 'off', suddenly it's all we pay attention to.

We may find ourselves pointing out to others the hangnail on our finger, looking at the redness around it, examining it, touching it over and over to see if it still hurts, getting salt in it that causes our eyes to water, or mindlessly playing with it. When it hurts, we become obsessed with it.

The same is true for a toothache, a sore muscle, and our thoughts.

When our thoughts are uncomfortable, we tend to get stuck on them, just as we adjust our attention onto whatever pain or discomfort our body may be experiencing.

Just because we have a toothache, it does not mean we are a tooth ache. It simply means we need to go to see a dentist to get it fixed. We can sit for hours, and mull it over, allow ourselves to feel fear, allow ourselves to think happy thoughts into the tooth, or call all of our friends and family to let them know that the tooth ache is there, or we can call the dentist to get it taken care of. When we get to the dentist, they will look at the tooth and determine the best course of action. They aren't going to ask how your tooth got to be this way, or what childhood experience with candy brought this into your experience now. They may ask 'when did you start to notice the pain', but most often, they will just see this is a problem, and get to work at fixing it.

    The same is true for our thoughts. We can sit for hours, and mull over them, allowing ourselves to believe that the thoughts are the truth. We can buy into the fear that comes up with them, we can try to wash the thought away by covering it in positive thoughts, or we can call all of our friends and family to let them know that the thoughts exist. We can sit and try to figure out where this thought is stemming from, what childhood experience it is connected to, but that may lead us down a rabbit hole of new thoughts coming up.

    The best course of action?

    Ask yourself: What triggered the thought in the first place? When did you notice it? How does it make you feel in your body? What emotions are attached to it?

Now all you have to do is sit and wait. The pain may become greater. The thought may get louder (just like a drill may seem very loud at the dentist.) You may find yourself scared to go through with the extraction of the thought (or tooth), and you may find that there is more pressure being put on you than you would like.

    It may take 10 minutes and it may take days to sit with the thought, to sit with the emotions and to truly hold space for yourself, as you allow yourself to see the thoughts that are coming up for you. Part of you may want to distract you from sitting with it, part of you may convince you to grab something to eat, part of you may roll it's eyes in exasperation that you need to just fucking do this!

As I stated earlier in the book, one of my own triggers to a tyranny of thoughts was when people would be dishonest. Another pattern of mine was triggered in another's silence. If they weren't talking a lot, I would assume that I had done something wrong, and my thoughts would take me for a couple of walks around the block, before I got the nerve to ask if I had done something wrong. (Typically the answer here was that I had done nothing wrong… the person was silent due to their own personal struggles, and it was not something for me to take personally at all).

Unless you are currently reading this book, being eaten by a tiger, or being transported from one place to another in the whirl wind of a tornado, I am going to assume that you are safe, right here, right now, in this moment. And yet, your thoughts may be making you feel unsafe, or worried about what you said yesterday in a meeting, or what the weekend's weather might be like.

Because the mind is meant to keep you safe, and the thoughts we have originate in our mind, the mind can become the creator of all of the worst-case-scenarios. And then it comes up with solutions for all of the worst-case-scenarios that it created in the first place. And then we get caught up in this cycle, of taking care of one imaginary problem, after another imaginary problem, by coming up with imaginary solutions for something that only exists in our mind.

It is the easiest way to keep ourselves distracted from the truth of what is in our hearts, and allow ourselves to get caught up in a web of lies in the mind.

Repeat after me:

Just because I think it, doesn't mean that it is true.
That's right.
Just because I think it, doesn't mean that it is true.

Our thoughts are created through our experiences, what we have been told (based on someone else's experience) and how those experiences made us feel.

It doesn't make any thought truthful, but rather, it shows just how easily we can manipulate our thoughts, or be distracted by them based on what our experiences were.

For example, you can take two people from two different backgrounds, and life experiences and bring them into a new experience together. Let's say the experience is a trip to the zoo.

For person A, their life experience was one of adventure. While they have never been to a zoo, they have travelled the world, they were raised by two adoring parents, who were devoted to creating a great upbringing.

For person B, their life experience was very limited. They were raised by a single mom, and often spent their nights at home alone, while their mother worked. They didn't get out of their own neighborhood a whole lot, and often felt alone in their experience. While their mother was devoted to taking care of them by making sure the bills were paid, and person B was fed, when it came to nurturing the child, there was very little time left.

Now person A and person B are at the same zoo, seeing the same animals.

Person A's thoughts look something like this: *These animals are really cool. I remember when I saw a zebra in Africa. What a trip that was. Dad was so enthralled by the safari. I remember how scared mom was of the animals. That was funny. Look at how big the pens are. There's so much room for them to run. They are beautiful creatures. I wonder what the next animal will be that we see.*

Person B's thoughts look something like this: *Wow, I've never been to a zoo before. This is so cool! I wish mom could see it with me. She always worked so hard for me. Man, I should have brought her. That poor zebra. In there, all by itself. I wonder where its mother is. I wonder if it even knows who its father is. I wish I knew who my father was. Shit. Don't cry. This is supposed to be fun. I have to stop being such a baby. God, I'm so sensitive. Zoos are kind of stupid. Why would anyone want to see a caged animal? They should have free space to run. Its pen is so small. Maybe it just wants more room to run. It looks kind of sad and lonely.*

Whose thoughts are right? Who has the better perspective of the zebra's experience? Who has a better outlook on the zoo?

It's a trick question. Based on what we know about their upbringing, they are both right. And they are both wrong. Which brings us to the neutrality of it all.

Our thoughts are neither good nor bad. They simply are what they are. Thoughts. Based on our experiences. Those experiences then attach emotions to the thoughts, which makes us believe that the thoughts are good or bad, that we are good or bad for thinking those thoughts, and that we must do something or change something about ourselves in order to function as a normal human.

However, when you start to be aware of your thoughts, and allow yourself to see what experiences you had that led you to have these thoughts, you can begin to see what thoughts are distracting you from the truth of who you are.

And while the experience that you had is influencing your thoughts, you get to decide what truth you want to bring forward into this moment now.

For person B, their first thoughts were about how they had never been to a zoo before and how cool it was. Instantly, they went into a guilt trip that they should have brought their mother (based on the experience of them 'owing' their mother for her hard work), and then started to feel their own abandonment through the zebra's experience, at which point, they got angry at themselves for feeling the ways that they were feeling. In those moments, the thoughts took over, and began to shed some light where person B may need to do some healing work.

However, for a lot of us, when we have the thoughts that just start to run and run, and we have the emotions that start coming up, we shut down. We decide we are never going to a zoo again. We decide that we need to fight for the animal to be out in the wild. We tell everyone we meet that they shouldn't go to a zoo, particularly to the zebras, as it was such a bad experience. We may even write a review on social media to let everyone know just how awful it was.

Meanwhile, all the Ego was pointing out through all of the thoughts that were coming up, was that there were still parts of the ego that felt guilty for how hard mom worked, and that it wants to 'prove itself' as worthy of such hard work. The Ego is still feeling hurt by mom's overworking, and abandoned by dad's inability to be a part of person B's life.

The Ego doesn't want us to go out and change it in the world. The Ego wants us to change our own world. The Ego simply wants and needs to feel the feelings, and work through the experiences, where you become the adult to your child-self, and your earlier experiences.

When you take the time to sit with the thoughts, and be aware of what the thoughts actually are, you can then begin to ask yourself, 'What parts of these thoughts are true for me?'

More often than not, these thoughts are based on the past, and when we were disappointed or hurt in some way, or based on the future, and our fears for what that might (or might not) look like for us.

This is why Buddhist monks tell us to stay in the present. The present is the only thing that is actually the truth. Not yesterday, as it no longer exists. And not tomorrow, because it hasn't been created yet. All we have is this moment. And it's all we have ever had.

And yet, we end up losing the present moment because we are so fixated on the past or the future, or both simultaneously.

Working with my ego, and working with clients to help them with their own journey of falling in love with their ego brings me back to a question that is asked over and over again.

'How do I know when it's my heart and not my Ego/Mind that is talking?'

The answer is simple.

You feel the truth of it.

As you become witness to your thoughts, allow yourself to *feel* the thoughts in your body.

Does your body feel good when you think the thought? Does your body feel fear when you think the thought? Does it feel expansive or restrictive?

When I look back through my life, the times when I was absolutely certain of something being the right path for me, my heart felt expansive, and I felt everything was possible. On the other hand, there were times when I felt small, questioning everything, and unsure of the next steps. My thoughts were very fearful and full of lack.

Most times, we associate thoughts around fear as being very limiting.

However, the thought that fear is limiting is also a thought in itself. Like all thoughts, sometimes, they can be expansive and sometimes they can be limiting.

The week before I married my ex-husband, I was filled with doubt. We had a decent relationship, a child together, he was helping me to raise my first born. He was a good guy.

And yet, there was a nagging thought that I shouldn't be marrying him.

I joked to him that if the singer on Canadian Idol I wanted to win, didn't win, I was going to call off the wedding (he didn't find that amusing), and when my chosen pick didn't win, I thought, surely this was a sign.

I ignored it.

The day of the wedding came, and the fear and anxiety were strong.

When it came to the time of me walking down the aisle, I looked at the church lady and said, I don't think I can go through with this. It felt so clear to me in my body.

She looked at me, rolled her eyes, and said 'Too late sweetheart', adjusted my dress and sent me down the aisle.

As I walked down the aisle, I decided that she was right. It was too late to change my mind. The fears that were coming up were silly. I was just afraid of the next step. Not a big deal. My heart felt restricted, but I pushed forward, thinking this is just what it feels like on your wedding day.

Two years later, on our second wedding anniversary, I asked for a divorce.

The signs were there, showing up in my body, telling me this wasn't the way to go, but I ignored them.

If someone had said to me on the day of the wedding, 'Is this what your heart wants?' I'm not sure I would have chosen differently. I was so disconnected from my heart; from the sensations that it showed me when it was speaking up; and so caught up in the thoughts of what was expected of me, what I was supposed to want, and what I was supposed to do, that listening to my heart was the least of my worries.

I was more worried about proving myself to the world around me. I was so caught up in these expectations (both real and perceived) that I lost the connection with myself.

More recently, I was set to go away on a meditation retreat, in another country, all by myself. During the weeks leading up to the retreat, I was feeling both fear and excitement in my body.

One day, about a week before leaving, my fears became more heightened. I was suddenly picturing myself dying on the airplane, getting hijacked in the taxi, getting mauled by a mountain lion, or being murdered by someone while I was there.

Without any proof that this would happen, I began to type out instructions for my will, including all of my website login information, email passwords, and more, to ensure my family could close out any business transactions due to my inevitable death that was going to happen.

About half way through, I heard my heart say, 'Are you serious? We aren't about to die. We are about to transform.'

Rather than ignoring it, I decided to stop my will-creating, and sit down for a meditation.

I allowed the fear to show itself. But, when I saw it in my mind's eye, my whole body reverberated with joy. My mind didn't understand it at first: How could I possibly feel fear (of death at that) and still feel joyful and expansive?

As I sat longer, I was able to see that the fear wasn't death itself, but rather that my Ego was clinging on to the last bit of hope that I would continue to feed it the small story that had kept me safe for so long. And my heart was rejoicing. My heart didn't want me to be small, or to stay small any longer. It wanted me to expand my story, and start telling a new one. It wanted me to experience the freedom that was available to me.

It's been over a year since I went on that retreat. And all of the thoughts that I had about dying while I was there were completely unfounded, and honestly a waste of my time and energy.

And that's the thing with thoughts: they waste our time and energy when we let ourselves get caught up in them or believe that they must be our truth.

We have been taught to run on auto-pilot, following the thoughts, following the media, following the rules, and obeying our parents. We have been taught to play it safe, to stay small, and to live within our comfort zone. We have been taught to look for proof of our own demise, our own suffering, and our own faults.

If I hadn't heard my heart speak up that day, I might have gotten on the internet to find out how many murders happened in that area over the past year, I might have started to notice plane crashes on the news, I might have called a lawyer to notarize my will. Rather than enjoying the trip while I was on it, I might have allowed fear to control me, thinking I was about to die any moment.

Remember, our thoughts are created from our past experiences, or what we have been told by another's experience.

Our thoughts are the different voices of our Ego, sometimes disguised as our mother's voice, the voice of the news anchor, or a school bully. The Ego repeats these thoughts, based on its experience, to make sure that you stay safe, that you are accepted, loved and valued by the world around you.

When we allow our thoughts to run rampant through our minds, without noticing what has triggered them, or even the path that they are taking us down, we can get caught up in feelings of not being good enough, getting things wrong, feeling rejected, feeling unloved and so many more. This often results in feeling defensive, angry or offended.

Be patient with yourself and allow yourself to see the thoughts and emotions as they come up. Be witness to them, but don't become them. Just as you are not your tooth, or your hangnail, you are not your thoughts, your emotions, or even your experiences.

The more you practice the awareness of witnessing your thoughts, the more you will see patterns emerging that trigger the thoughts in the first place. It is in this awareness of your thoughts that you will begin to find the path to your own inner truth.

Heart Work:

For a day, keep a journal of your thoughts as they come into your awareness. If necessary, put an alarm on your phone for an hourly check in, where you can pause for 5 minutes and write down whatever thoughts that come forward for you.

When the day is over, take some time to reflect on what the thoughts are that came forward.

How many of your thoughts are truthful loving statements?

How many of your thoughts are based on fear about future experiences?

How many of your thoughts are based on disappointment or hurt from past experiences?

How many of your thoughts are connected to another person's experience and how they view you?

If you had thoughts that were connected to another person's experience, or to a future event, did any of those thoughts become a reality since you first had the thought (or became aware of the thought?)

Do the thoughts make you feel good, bad, uncomfortable or neutral?

Chapter # 8

Dancing with Anger

At the beginning of the year, I stated to my husband that I wanted to get to the root of my anger. I was done with boiling under the surface and wanted to use my inner flame to turn on my light.

I was pissed at a lot of things; external experiences that kept knocking me off course; I was pissed at the world and the chaos that kept happening; I was pissed at injustices, cowardness and fears. I was pissed at the people who were causing it all. I was pissed at myself for not being able to heal it all. I was pissed at myself for being pissed.

Of course, when you make a statement like *show me the root of my anger* the Universe says 'here, let us show you. Let us trigger you. Let us help you feel your anger. Let us help you find your voice in your anger.'

And then the Universe releases a cosmic shit show on your angry heart.

And guides you at the same time.

'Here,' the Universe whispers. 'Your anger is not the enemy.... your resistance to it for the past 10000 years is the enemy... the block. Just feel it. Let it rage through you.'

'Here' the Universe leads you. 'I'm going to put you in situations that make you uncomfortable. I'm going to put you in challenging situations. Some will make you lash out, some will make you cry, and some will challenge you to rise above. Remember that whatever your reaction, they are all okay.'

'Still not getting it?' The Universe sighs. 'Here, let us trigger you. Let us trigger your past hurts, let us trigger the inner child, the abandoned, the broken and the bruised parts of you. From this lifetime, from previous lifetimes. From your family line, and the family lines of your ancestors. You have the permission to feel ALL that has been pushed down, told to shut up and told to calm down. Feel it all now.'

'Ahhh, you're getting it now,' the Universe whispers. 'Breathe. Remain calm. Use your triggers to see your boundaries. Use your voice to set them. Yes, it's scary. But do it anyway. I won't leave you. Some might. But I won't. You're safe with me.'

'You see,' the Universe holds me, 'Your anger has been showing you where you have been neglecting your voice, your boundaries, and most importantly your soul. Your anger is one step from your passion.'

Continuing, the Universe says, 'When you dance with your anger, when you feel it, you will find your Self; your purpose; your mission.'

'All of the anger you have to those not taking responsibility for their actions? Take responsibility for yours. Teach others to do it. Take away the shame and guilt about being human. Take away the judgement.'

'All of the anger you have to those not doing the work, teach others to do their own work. Find a way to teach that takes away the struggle that you have experienced.'

'All of the anger that you have for not having a voice in external experiences, use that to bring voice to your own internal experience.'

'Use your anger as a lighthouse for others. Dance with your anger to create your passion'.

Chapter # 9

The Great Undoing

As we become more aware of the thoughts that we have, the emotions that they trigger, and how they either limit or expand us into our existence, we can begin what I like to call the 'Great Undoing'.

This is the undoing of all of our limiting beliefs, stories, experiences, thoughts, and feelings that we have picked up along the way, and stored nicely in our backpacks of life, as though they will one day be useful.

Humans across the globe want to feel as though they fit in, fit the mold, and are accepted. At the same time, humans across the globe want to be noticed, seen, and feel heard in their existence.

And yet, most often, we put on the masks that we believe we need to be wearing in order for others to accept us. In our striving to be accepted by others, we reject the authenticity that we bring to the table, and then feel as though we are still being rejected (because WE are the ones rejecting OURSELVES).

One of my favorite quotes is *'Aerodynamically, the bumble bee can't fly, but it doesn't know that, so it goes on flying anyway'* - Mary Ann Kash.

I heard this when I was a kid, and it filled me with such joy to think that a bumble bee, of all things, could break the laws of physics, and do what it felt necessary, regardless of what others thought about it.

It was later in my adult years that I found out that new scientific research realized that due to a closer study of the bee, and new understanding of physics, actually proved that the bumble bee knew it could fly the entire time, and was built to do exactly that.

Now imagine, if when Mary Ann Kash made her statement about the bumble bee, that the bumble bee had heard that, and was like, 'Shit, really? Damn, I'll stop flying then. Sorry! Didn't mean to step on any toes'.

Regardless of what it knew to be true (the proof was in the fact that the bumble bee had been flying for centuries) the bumble bee would have stopped flying, and life, as we know it, would be over.

Now from Mary Ann's perspective, and knowledge of physics at the time, and how the bumble bee was built, this quote was true. But as time went on, and new information was revealed, it turned out that it wasn't true at all.

And that's what the Great Undoing is all about.

Our parents, our educators, our friends, our news sources, our government leaders, and we, all live within the perspective of what we know to be true.

Our parents may have witnessed themselves, their parents or even their friends really struggle to get a business off the ground, and so in their experience, they may squash your own ideas of building a business as it is too hard from their perspective.

Our friends may have stayed in a relationship despite wanting desperately to be out of it, and warn you about the dangers of leaving your own relationship, because they are afraid to leave theirs.

We ourselves may have had to do an oral presentation in class when we were younger, and messed up on our words, and refuse to do any public speaking now as adults for fear of the embarrassment to happen again.

The big question you have to ask yourself is how many of my thoughts, and experiences of reality are actually my truth, and how many of them are what I have been told to believe as truth?

It's important as well to recognize that this isn't a blame game against anyone who has taught us what we believe (or think we need to believe), but rather is an opportunity for you to become more self-aware of what is actually true for you.

The Great Undoing isn't an overnight activity, but rather a constant evaluation of what you believe to be true, or not. It's putting all of the pieces together that fit the puzzle that is you.

When I was a child, my parents were not very religious. They didn't attend church, or do any spiritual practices that I was aware of. My father had walked away from his own religious upbringing, and swore that he would never return.

When I was about seven or eight years old, I started to attend a Mennonite church with my grandparents. They were longstanding members at the church, and my grandmother was very devoted to her religion and beliefs.

This was my first taste of God and my first taste of spirituality.

My parents didn't argue with my desire to go to church, however, they did state more than once that they didn't understand my desire to go. For myself, I loved it, and loved to learn about God and the Bible. While some of the teachings almost put me to sleep, every once in a while I would get a nugget that made me feel so good, that I would want to go back.

In my early teen years, after family issues arose due to my grandfather's actions, I stopped attending church with my grandparents.

Still longing for a new church, I joined a church

choice at a local Presbyterian church, and used the choir as an excuse to continue to go to church.

In many ways, I felt guilty for still wanting a church, and a connection to God, especially after my grandfather's sexual abuse was revealed. *How could a man of God do such a thing? Did I even want to be a religious person? Not like that!*

While I wasn't listening as much to the teachings as much as I was singing, I continued to study the Bible on my own time, trying to understand the language and apply it to my life. By the time I went into high school, I left behind my Bible, and started to experience life first hand, rather than trying to find the answers in some book.

Later in my teen years, my older sister and her husband introduced me to their church. They offered to 'save me'. I started to attend with them every Sunday, and tried to join the youth group.

The first week went well. I felt a bit out of place, but everyone was doing their best to help me feel welcome.

The following week, I needed a ride, and was promised a ride from one of the other members of the group. Sitting around for a couple of hours waiting, I realized that he wasn't going to be picking me up. I was disappointed, but it didn't ruin my night.

The following day I was told that he was worried that he may do something 'violent and sexual' if he had picked me up, so he used his better judgement and left me at home.

Well, thank God for that!

The whole religious thing didn't seem to be working out for me very well.

As years went by, I found myself looking for more answers, for a deeper connection. Rather than looking in churches, I started to read books, and invest more in self-help and spirituality.

There were many opportunities for me to step away from my truth and the deeper calling that was within me. There were many around me who were more than willing to share their own lack of belief with me; many who were willing to show me how religion worked in their own experience; and many who were ready to judge me if I didn't follow the rules of their religion.

My own truth shone through all of that. I never did believe that God was there to make me suffer; I never did believe that I should be punished for my sins. I never believed that I was better than another for attending church, or that I, as a woman, didn't have a right to speak up in the church.

And while others were telling me that these were the truth that I must buy into, the rebellious part of me wouldn't have any of it.

I wasn't always so lucky with my truth leading the way. In fact, more often than not, my own truth wasn't even present in the moment, but rather tucked way far way so I could be accepted at the time.

The older I get, the more I realize that this is how it has been for so many of us.

We are not taught to question what we are being told, we are not taught to seek out the information for ourselves, and see what resonates and what doesn't. We are told to keep our mouths shut, listen, obey, and follow through. Stay within the lines, think within the box. Be who you are, but not so much that it makes others ask questions.

This can be a good thing: being taught to not steal from others, to drive following the rules, how to read and write properly are all essential for us to function in society.

However, sometimes, we are better off to question

what we are being told. Sometimes, based on their own limited perspectives, the people that love us and want the best for us, are only passing along their own limitations.

As teenagers, we do tend to navigate these paths on our own and rebel against what our parents are telling us.

But when we are younger, we believe the words we are being told as being the actual truth. We believe that our parents reactions to our behavior are dictating our worth, our belonging and how much love we deserve.

It is through these actions and reactions that we begin to lose ourselves, in our plight to feel loved, and to not be rejected by our parents, or the world around us.

When we give ourselves the opportunity to observe the thoughts that keep replaying in our minds, we also give ourselves the opportunity to question what is our truth and what is not. We can also begin to see what stories we have bought into, what beliefs we have that belonged to our parents, or other authority figures in our lives, and what we want to do with them now.

After I asked my husband for a divorce, I started to break away all of the pieces of me that were no longer my truth (or I was no longer accepting as being my truth). I started to question my life, my purpose, my experiences, and my feelings and emotions that were tied to all of those.

In doing that, I began to find deeper levels of truth, of who I was, and who I am now. I say began, because back then, only so much was revealed. Over time, deeper and deeper truths began to reveal themselves, and as I sit here now, writing about it, I know there are even deeper truths that will be revealed to me, perhaps later today, perhaps tomorrow. I'm never sure of the 'when' but I know they will happen.

Part of my undoing was letting go of the expectations

of others. Now understand that some of these were expectations that I perceived to be there, even though they weren't (as I later found out). Some of them were expectations that others did place on me, that left them feeling disappointed that I wasn't following through any longer with the narrative that they had written.

Was it scary?

Absolutely!

It is scary as fuck!

When you decide to discover your own truth, and listen to the still voice within, it can feel like your entire life is falling apart.

Is it worth it then?

Absolutely!

Your journey to discovering yourself and your own truths is a very personal one.

Imagine that you were stuck in a dark room for days on end, with absolutely no light. Suddenly you hear a few bangs outside of the room, and you get excited. Someone is about to save you. You brace yourself in anticipation. They open an unseen door, and suddenly the room is blasted with light. Your eyes sting from the brightness. You may have to shield them until you adjust to the light that is coming in. It's not that the light is too bright, or that the light needs to change, it's simply because you have been in the dark so long that you need to some to adjust to this new normal.

It is very much the same in the Great Undoing. At first, as you discover that maybe not everything you have been told to believe or do or become starts to surface, you brace yourself in anticipation. You are about to save yourself from the darkness that you've been caught up in. And then a lightbulb goes off: You suddenly realize that you have been following a paradigm that keeps you limited and stuck. And while you are excited to be rescued from your own limitations, it hurts. The truth of who you are can feel too big, too bright. It doesn't mean that it's wrong, or needs to change, but you may need some time to adjust to the brightness of your being.

The first step is to get honest with yourself about the choices and decisions you have made in your life up until this point. You still have to be accountable for these choices, as they are what you decided on, however, start to break down what made you make the choices.

Did you make the choices because they were truly what you wanted in the moment? Did you choose them because that's what your parents told you to choose? Did your friends approve of your partner, so you stayed with them? Were you more worried about paying the bills than whether you were actually happy at the dead end job? Were you afraid of losing your family if you followed the path or desire that kept coming up for you?

The greatest example of disregarding your own truth comes forward in this digital age. I am usually pretty good with directions, and often can figure out the best path to take by simply looking at a map.

A few months ago, I was invited to a friend's cottage for the weekend, and as I was only able to leave for the cottage after dark, I decided to turn on my GPS to get there.

At one point, the GPS started to take me in a direction that just felt wrong. I turned the way that I wanted to go, but the GPS wouldn't re-route, and continued to tell me to turn around. Eventually I did, and what was to be a 1.5 hour drive turned into almost 3 hours. The GPS led me the longest way possible to the cottage. I got there late, tired, hungry and pissed off that I hadn't followed my own truth and what my body was telling me.

Although my heart knew that it wasn't the right choice, my thoughts were worried that it was possibly a sign from the Universe that this was the best path; that I would be in a car accident if I didn't follow the GPS; that I would get lost in the middle of nowhere, and spend my entire night there; that I would run out of gas... the list went on and on.

None of them were true. Or perhaps all of them were. I will never know, as I chose to just listen to what the GPS said, rather than my own inner GPS- my intuition.

And this is the incredible part of the human existence. We get to choose, multiple times a day, what direction we want to take, what ways we want to live our life, and who we are wanting to please.

So often we are caught up in trying to please others, just as I had chosen to please the GPS, and we get angry and frustrated at how much longer everything seems to take, and we grow tired and weary (and hungry too!) from a road that has been travelled too long.

The Great Undoing allows you to bypass all of that, by taking away all of the other noise and distraction, and bringing yourself back to the truth of who you are, and what holds true in your heart.

As you get more honest with yourself, you may start to find the humor in it all. The ways that you have always done things, the paths that you have chosen, may have had nothing to do with you at all.

I remember one story I heard a few years back, of a woman who was learning how to make a sauce that was handed down by her grandmother. Her mother was teaching it to her. Half of the ingredients went into one pot, and half of the ingredients went into another pot. They were both cooked separately, and then later served together.

After making the recipe a few times, and wondering

why they were being cooked separately, she asked her mother, 'Why do we do it like this? Why not just use a bigger pot?'

The mother replied that it was just the way she had been taught and she never questioned it.

The next time the woman seen her grandmother, she asked her, 'Why do we do it like this?'

The grandmother replied that when she was a child, her parents didn't have a lot of money for big expensive pots, and so the mother just made the recipe in two separate pots. She had never thought of just using a bigger pot. She just did it the same way her mother had taught her.

When we don't question what we have been taught, and accept it as just being the way it is, we may find ourselves doing twice the amount of work for the same results. When we start to question it, we may begin to realize that even though that was the way it was done in the past, it doesn't mean that it's the way it needs to continue to be.

It may not always feel safe to do things differently, or even to ask questions about why we need to do things in a certain way, or behave a certain way.

Remember the Ego's purpose is to make sure you stay safe, and aren't hurt in anyway. So questioning what is your truth and what is not, means the Ego may very well start to act up and try to get you to close the lid on it, rather than dive into it further.

Pay attention to the fears that come up and the thoughts that are playing out as you begin to question everything, and step into the Great Undoing. The way you're your Ego is reacting could very well be why you have been not following your truth this entire time.

When my ego started to react to me not following the GPS a lot of my fears and thoughts were focused on being alone, and being lost. And even though I was on a very well-lit highway, the fears felt very real.

When I looked closer at this, and my own realizations of being abandoned or being alone in life events, I realized again, that the thoughts were trying to protect me from feeling the abandonment that I had felt before, just under a new narrative, and a new experience.

But again, just because it's kept us safe in the past, doesn't mean that it is the only way for us to live.

We have to question. We have to have a curiosity within ourselves to look at every situation with new eyes, not tainted by the past, or the expectations, or other people. As much as I want you to eat up every single word that I am writing as being the gospel, I also want you to question it all, and figure out your own truths as you are reading through. I want you to have a thirst of curiosity that even when you think you have found your own answer, that you are willing to open yourself to something even deeper.

It is through our questioning, and through our curiosity that we can begin to listen to the callings of our heart, and the purpose of our Soul. It is through our questions that we can develop a deeper awareness of who we are on so many different levels, and accept ourselves for who we are and how we think and how we behave at a deeper level.

Every day is an opportunity for us to go through the Great Undoing and allow us to step back into our truth... the person we were, before the limitations and expectations. The one who believed in him or herself. The one that believed (s)he could be anyone or anything that she wanted to be. The one that trusted that (s)he was more than enough.

You may not remember them. But they're there. I promise you.

Heart Work:

Grab your journal and write down any experiences you had when you were aware that it wasn't what you wanted to do, and yet you went ahead and did it anyway. What were you feeling as you did it? How did it feel in your body? Now that you are no longer in that experience, what feelings come up for you when you think about that experience? Who or what were you trying to please by choosing that experience?

Looking back at that experience, what do you wish you had done differently? Why didn't you do that at the time? What were you afraid of happening if you did choose differently?

Is there any patterns that you can see (word choice, feelings, emotions, or thoughts) that are coming up for you that are connected to the way your Ego feels?

What triggers are being revealed to you by looking back at these choices?

How can you choose your truth now?

Chapter # 10

Rediscovering Your Self

As you begin your great undoing, you may find yourself getting caught up in the past, and the experiences that you have had.

While the past is revealing to you where your truths lie, and what has kept you from those truths, make no mistake: your past is exactly what it had to be.

Your upbringing, experiences, relationships, choices, and thoughts have all created the you that exists today. They may not have always been fun, enlightening or even enjoyable. They may have taken you down paths that later regretted, or they may have broken your heart repeatedly. This doesn't mean that they were wrong.

(Disclaimer: This does not mean that if you were someone who experienced abuse of any kind, addictions, etc., that THAT was right either! That is a whole different conversation for an entirely different book.)

So often when we look at our past, we focus on the mistakes, and then judge ourselves for not being further ahead than what we are currently at.

But the truth is, we only know what we know at the time. We do the best that we can with the information that we have on hand at that moment, and then use our best judgement to make a choice. In hindsight, the older, wiser person that we become can look back at it and decide that there was definitely a better way. But when we were younger, we weren't that older, wiser person. So cut yourself a break.

Even now, as an older wiser person, you may choose something that in five years from now, you look back at and wonder why you would make such a choice. And again, it comes back to what you know to be true now.

We are constantly evolving and changing as a species. We only know what we know, until we know something different, and then we know that.

As we begin our conversations with the Ego, and we begin to heal the past hurts and pains, we must be willing to accept our part in them, without criticism or judgement, knowing that we were simply doing the best that we knew how to do at that time.

As more information is revealed to us, we may change our minds, or choose a different path. And that is okay too.

For so many (I and my clients included) every choice we make we think is this lifelong commitment. And so we stand in fear, afraid of making the wrong choice. It's almost as though we believe it is the last choice we could ever possibly make. And we create it to be bigger and bigger in our minds, rather than just simply looking at it as just a choice that we are making in the moment.

Quite often it is shame and guilt of our past choices, or the ways others have reacted to our past choices, that make us so afraid to screw it all up again.

Imagine the freedom in telling yourself that whatever choice you made in the past was perfect, and whatever choice you make today is going to be perfect as well. Imagine the freedom in believing, that no matter what, no matter your choice, no matter your vision, no matter the final destination that you're going to do it brilliantly?

What would you choose then?

Would you continue to choose what you're currently choosing, or would you choose something differently altogether? Would you take a chance on yourself or would you play it small?

Here's a secret:

There's no way for you to fuck this up.

Sure, you may fall; you may fail; the relationship may break down; the plan may not go accordingly- but who you are; the you that created the plan in the first place, took the chance, strived for success, opened your heart to love; it's still going to be here.

How do I know that?

Because we are all still here now.

Even with all of the mistakes of the past; even with the heart ache; the pain, the messes; we are all still here, striving for something better, striving to know ourselves deeper, and striving to be better than we were yesterday.

So really, there is no way for you to fuck this up.

Your Soul knows this at the deepest level. Your Soul has been on Earth countless times, trying, failing, loving and hurting, lifetime after lifetime; and yet it still comes back, looking for more of this good human-ness to experience again.

The Ego on the other hand believes everything is life or death. But the only part of you that is truly dying every time you take a chance on yourself, is the part of your Ego that didn't believe that you deserved it in the first place.

Which takes us back to the past.

Because the Ego was created at a time when you were young, naïve, and didn't have a lot of choice but to listen to the adults around you, and also didn't have the emotional support system (or the function in the brain to deal with emotions appropriately at the time) the Ego will consistently show up with the idea of doom and gloom and hopelessness. It's not that it wants to hurt you, but it's been hurt and disappointed enough in the past, to know that being hurt or disappointed just sucks.

And we can't blame it for that either.

Just as we can't shame our past, or guilt ourselves for the choices that we have made, it's important that don't get caught up in the idea that Ego is a bad thing, or something for us to be shameful of, or guilty for having.

After all, the Ego got us through some of our toughest experiences, when we were too small to understand. If anything, it deserves a whole lot of love for doing what it could to protect us in the best way that it knew how to at the time.

As we begin to dismantle our untruths, and we step more so into the truth of who we are, we may find the Ego starting to get louder, or reacting in bigger ways when we are being triggered.

Again, cut yourself, and the Ego some slack.

The rediscovering of the self is a process, and like all of the other work that I've talked about in this book, it's not an overnight step that will fix your entire world the next day. It's a journey, a commitment that you make to yourself every day, as you reconnect with your own truths, and allow yourself to let go of what is no longer you (and sometimes wasn't even you in the first place).

Uncovering the thoughts that got us here, the belief systems that helped to mold us, and the emotions that we have held onto that are no longer serving a purpose is all a part of the process.

When I first started to write this book, I had an idea in my mind of what it was to look like, and what information I needed to share. But as with all journeys, the book started to take on a life of its own. There were weeks when I wouldn't even open it on my computer, and days where I would stay up until the wee hours of the morning working on it. The more I was working on creating my own relationship with Kevin, the more the book began to shift. When I started I only knew what I knew, and as time went on, the knowing started to shift, and the awareness grew bigger.

It wasn't that I wasn't ready when I first started the book, but rather, I was opening myself to the journey of discovering what the book would be about, while also paying attention to the shifts that would be happening in my life as I wrote.

Where ever you are on your journey as you are reading this is perfect. Some of my insights may be hitting you like a ton of bricks, and some of them may be reminders for things that you already know, but need to remember.

In life, we are so quick to judge ourselves on the journey that we are on. We tend to go along, picking up all of these different methods of self-awareness, self-love and spiritual growth, placing them one by one in our backpack of knowledge, and then we forget about them, or forget to practice them, or practice them for a bit, see that they work, and promptly stop doing them. And then we judge ourselves some more, when life gets tough, and we realize we haven't been doing all of the things that we know how to do.

When we become gentle with ourselves, when we allow ourselves to accept where we are at any given moment as being the perfect place, the perfect emotion, the perfect reaction, we give ourselves the room and space for the growth to happen.

However, if we are harsh with ourselves, if we get mad, ashamed or even guilty for where we are at, for what we are feeling, for how we are reacting, we are only going to stay in the same spot.

After all, you catch more flies with honey than you do with vinegar.

Psychologists and parenting experts have been studying for years the proper way to raise a child, the proper way to discipline, and the effects of trauma, abuse and more on the developing child's brain. And we recognize that the child must be loved and nurtured, and feel accepted for who they are and what they are doing and creating in their life, while also offering guidance on making the right choices.

Regardless of what age you currently are, you are every age, at any given moment, that you have ever been. You may even be multiple ages all at the same time in this moment. Even though you are an adult, you need to feel loved, nurtured, accepted for who you are, what you are doing and what you are creating in your life, while also following guidance on how to make the right choices for you.

When you start to put expectations on yourself for where you are, how much you've done, what you know, what you don't know, what you're applying and what you're not, you are left with a whole mixed bag of emotions, and a feeling of just not being good enough, or getting it right yet.

Imagine a child who always got D's in school. They may feel as though they are not smart, or that their best just isn't good enough, and they try harder to get a better grade. When they bring home a C, the parents have two choices. Either celebrate the C, or reprimand the child for not getting an A. What choice do you think would support the child more?

The choice may be obvious to celebrate the C, however, when it comes to how we treat ourselves, we often expect the A immediately. We may think, I've read these books, I've done this healing work, I've forgiven the past, why am I just not getting an A yet? Why am I only getting a C?

It's not always about getting the A though. Sometimes it's about getting the C or B. Sometimes it's about getting the D, and seeing where you went wrong, and learning more about what you still need to learn, what answers you have difficulty with, and how you react to being tested. That's where the real growth starts to happen.

As you are rediscovering yourself, you are unlearning everything that wasn't working for you in the first place. As you are rediscovering yourself, you're understanding yourself at a deeper level, understanding your triggers, your thought patterns, your conditional thinking, your fears, your pains. It's not an overnight delivery of 'just getting it' or a 'one stop shop' to heal all the shit from your past.

When you give yourself the memo that it's all trial and error, you free yourself from any expectations that you have placed on yourself (or picked up from someone else that you're comparing yourself to) that you need to get it perfected the first time around.

I learned this lesson hard this past year.

I have been working on my anger for quite some time. I am usually pretty happy-go-lucky, full of positivity and calm. But every once in a while, anger boils up, and when it does, it can be quite scary, for myself, and those that I am projecting it on.

I started the year off saying I needed to get to the source of my anger, so that I had more control over it, than it did of me.

Things were going fine.

And then one day I snapped.

I appointed myself to be a driver for my step-dad to get to and from appointments as he were being prepared for surgery. The day of his surgery, they wanted to get there early in the morning, so I set my alarm for 3am. I got up, got ready, picked up my sister, and then went to pick up him and my mom.

That morning they were in a high state of emotion. He were going to get his kidney taken out as a tumor had been discovered. They were both nervous, and understandably so.

As we got on our way, there was some construction at an intersection. I wasn't able to bypass the construction and had to wait for some vehicles to pass that were coming from the other way. The family member made some snide comments about how I needed to get going. They didn't want to be late. I assured them we wouldn't be late. We had left two and a half hours early for a one hour drive.

I turned at the intersection, only to be met with yelling, as I had taken the wrong direction. I was supposed to go straight through. Again, I took a calm breath, apologized, pulled into a parking lot, turned around and we go on our way.

As we drove, the tension was high. He continued to make small remarks, about things that were happening in the world and in our family. In my mind, I was thinking, this better not be the way this entire trip is going to go, or I will lose my mind.

Part of me was able to recognize that it was his own fears that were causing his hostility, part of me wanted to smack him back into reality that I was doing him a favor and in no way deserved to be yelled at for helping him out.

When we arrived at the hospital there was an

emergency situation out front where a patient was being detained by police, doctors and nurses. I couldn't pull in to the main entrance as I had in the past as the entrance was blocked by police cars.

I pulled into the parking lot, where we sat for about 45 minutes, waiting for his surgery time to come so he could go into the hospital. (This took place during the Covid-19 pandemic and no one was allowed to be in the hospital with him).

When the time for his surgery came, we drove back over to the main entrance, but the police cars were still there. I slowed down a bit to see if I could bypass them and get closer to the hospital door. I wasn't able to, so I pulled into the next driveway to turn around.

I hadn't realized it at the time but it was a one way entry and I pulled in, in the wrong direction.

It wasn't a big deal. I had to make a 3 point turn and would be able to turn around.

But all hell broke loose.

He started to yell at me, 'What the hell are you doing? Are you stupid? It's a one way! Why did you pull in here?'

And that was the straw that broke the camel's back. All of my calmness, all of my forgiveness went right out the window.

I reacted badly. "You know what?! Shut the fuck up! I woke up early, I drove you down here, and yes, I've made a few fucking mistakes, and I'm sorry for that, but appreciate what I am doing for you! I'm turning around. You're not going to be late. I get that you're scared but you don't get to fucking speak to me like this!' I yelled.

Shame came over me. I apologized, "I'm sorry. I get that you're nervous but I don't deserve to be…"

At that he started to yell. I'm not even sure what he said at this point. There was a lot of fuck you bitch, and other curse words. He told me to never speak to him again. To not pick him up.

I knew without a doubt I had messed up, but the more I listened to him scream at me, belittle me and curse at me, I knew in some odd way that I had done the right thing, to stand up for myself. It had been a time bomb waiting to go off.

The entire ride home my mom was silent. My sister made small chat. Inside I was gutted. It wasn't the way that I wanted to react. I felt ashamed, guilty, and hurt by his reaction, and my mom's lack of reaction to the whole thing.

When we got home, I cried, and cried, and then cried some more. Speaking to my husband and a close friend, they both agreed with me that I had a right to be hurt, to feel hurt, and to have spoken up for myself.

"I was supposed to be over this anger though. I was supposed to be a support system for my mom this time around. When my dad had cancer I was awful. This time was supposed to be better," I told them both.

"You were never supposed to be a support system for your mom when you were 15," my friend told me. "You needed support. You had a right to be angry then, and you have a right to be angry now."

The words hit me hard.

Through the cancer scare that my step-dad was having, I had devoted myself to being there for my mom. As much as I had worked on myself, and my own healing, one part that I was still carrying and holding onto was the guilt and shame for the way I had acted out when my dad was diagnosed with cancer.

My own father's cancer diagnosis had put me in a tail

spin. I started to smoke cigarettes, became promiscuous, acted out with bursts of anger, tried to run away from home, and attempted to commit suicide eight times within five months. On one particular night, I had told my father I hated him. On another I spent an evening standing in the front hallway, crying and hyperventilating. Three weeks before he died, I found out I was pregnant, which would later turn into a molar pregnancy. I was a royal fuck-up.

When my dad was in a morphine-induced coma, three days before he passed, I sat with him and apologized to him for my behavior since he had been diagnosed. He couldn't say anything, but for a brief moment he opened his eyes and simply stared at me. That moment always stood out to me. In the simplest of ways, I felt that it meant that he forgave me.

After his passing, life started to fall apart even more. I had the molar pregnancy, got into a fist fight with my best friend, and got kicked out of my house. My mom, dealing with her own depression from my father's death, and her inability to cope with my defiant behavior, had enough.

As the years went on, my mom and I were able to forge a new relationship with one another. But I would often hear comments, from her, and her new husband about what a bad kid I had been.

I eventually started speaking up about how I wasn't a bad kid, but more so, I was a troubled kid, who didn't know how to cope with what life was giving her. The 'bad kid' label was dropped, but after my blow up on the day of the surgery, it came back with a flourish.

Suddenly, I was that bad kid again. Suddenly, regardless of how much growth and commitment I had made to healing myself, it all went out the window, because I had a burst of anger.

When my friend told me that I had a right to be angry and it was not my job to support my mother like I hadn't been able to when I was a kid, I realized that it was not my father who I needed to forgive me.

It was me who needed to forgive me. I had spent so long trying to 'prove' that I was no longer that 'bad kid'. That came with a lot of good things; the work I do for others, and the work that I have done for myself; the books that I have written, the work that I have created and the lives that I have changed. That also came with a lot of baggage of needing to 'prove myself', of 'not feeling as though I deserved anything good', of 'not being good enough'.

I also realized that as much as I had been working with Kevin and all of the emotions that Kevin had experienced around my dad's death, the one area that I hadn't even looked at was the abandonment that I had felt in my mom's reaction to me when I couldn't handle the world that I was experiencing.

I had been focusing on the feeling of abandonment in my father's death. I had simply made excuses for my mom, and the ways that she had abandoned me when I needed her, so much so, that as an adult, I tried to fix the mistakes I had made as a teenager by becoming the support system for her that I couldn't be when I was younger. The messed up part about it all was that I was the one who had needed the support from her, not the other way around.

So I could give myself a D on this test and then guilt myself for getting a D (which I was doing initially). However, in that 'D', I came to a new level of awareness of understanding my own pain, my own patterns of guilt and shame, and a new level of understanding my feelings of abandonment. I was able to start healing at a whole new level, and to cry out the pain that I had been holding onto in my body for over twenty years.

Sometimes we take five steps forward, and six steps back. Sometimes we are only able to see one level of pain because it's all we can handle at the time. Sometimes, we need to step backwards, in order to move forward again. And sometimes, we need to revert back to the old pain, and the old ways of dealing with that pain, to understand it at a deeper level.

Healing isn't about getting it perfect.

Healing is about bringing yourself to a new level of understanding of why you do the things that you do, while loving yourself for acting or behaving that way. It's an open door of forgiveness that is available to you at all times.

Yes, it may be about forgiving other people, but more often than not, it's about forgiving yourself for dealing with your emotions in the best way that you can at any given moment.

Because at times, your best will be a calm breath taken and a mouth kept shut, and other times, your best will be you self-combusting and spewing angry words over anyone around you.

You may have moments where you are at both ends of the spectrum, and times when you're in a new dimension of emotions all together.

And it's all okay.

Wherever you are, it's perfect. Whatever emotions you have, whatever reactions you have, whatever experiences you have, they are all a part of a big picture to help you get back to the 'you' that was there before all of the shit happened.

Chapter # 11

Blind Spots

We all have blind spots, no matter how long we have been on the healing journey, no matter how long we have been at it, and how much we have uncovered, or recovered from.

Like myself, one of my greatest blind spots was looking at my dad's death as being the source of feelings of abandonment, rather than looking at the rest of the experience, and the abandonment that came out of it. My dad's death was only one small aspect of everything I lost that year, and only one small part of me that needed to heal through the years.

Our blind spots usually develop around the same time as the bigger experiences that have caused us pain. Sometimes we put them all in one bag together, with the focus being the 'main event' rather than all of the other events that happened because of the main event.

The main event is easy to spot. The main event is life changing- a death, a job loss, a divorce.

We may refer to the main event(s) in our life as 'before my divorce' and 'after my divorce', 'before his death', and 'after his death', or 'before the car accident' and 'after the car accident'.

Whatever follows the 'before' and 'after' are the main event; the area that you look at as being the central point of your pain, and the central point of where the healing needs to happen.

The blind spot though is the build up to the main event, and what happened when the main event was over.

One client of mine experienced a house fire when she was five years old. The fire was the main event. Family members died in the fire. After the fire, her father turned to alcohol to deal with his pain. Her mother started to have affairs. She dealt with a lot of anger and hurt. She mourned the loss of her siblings, felt guilt for her own life, and anger at the loss of both of her parents, even though they were both alive. Her father's alcoholism, her mother's cheating, and her own guilt were all blind spots that wasn't able to look at. They were the after-effects of the fire, but for her, she was only seeing the fire as the cause of her pain.

Another client discovered her husband has been having an affair for years when he told her he was filing for divorce so he could marry his mistress. She looked at the affair as being the main event. But upon further conversation, she discovered that the blind spots had been there for quite some time. She felt neglected in the relationship for years, had stopped putting in any effort for date nights, sex, or even conversation. They had become roommates.

She had been so focused on healing her feelings of rejection in regards to the affair, and in her words, getting nowhere. As we began to work together, she was able to see the rejection she had been feeling for years start to make itself known. The more she discovered, the more were being revealed, but in the realization of all of the emotions coming to the surface, she started to feel the weight of her burdens starting to shift.

When we are dealing with the main events of our lives, it can be easy to get caught up in the emotions and shock of what the main event is, but quite often, there are so many emotions that happen before and after, and if we are living in a state of shock of the events, we don't give ourselves the open space to process or heal them.

There is always a buildup that leads to the main event, or an unravelling that happens when the main event is over and done with.

The Ego remembers the main event. I does remember the blind spot events as well, but because the pain is greater with the main event, it may lead you to bypass the blind spots as the emotional pain is centralized on the main event.

When this happens, it can be harder for us to heal all of it. And if you're anything like me, you'll get on a hamster wheel, spinning and spinning on the same track, and wondering why you're not getting any different results. You can heal the main event as many times as you want, but until you start looking at the before and after, the buildup and the fall apart, you will only keep spinning.

This doesn't mean that your healing of the main event has gone unnoticed, but rather, that the main event was only one part- you also need to look at all of the smaller events that happened as you got closer to the main event, or after the main event happened.

Quite often the blind spots have the same energy and emotions attached to them as what the main event did. In the case of my father's death, I felt abandoned by him, however, in looking further into the blind spots and the energy and emotions that were connected to his death I was suddenly able to see so many more areas where the feelings of abandonment had also been.

The feeling of abandonment was seeded when my parents kicked me out for three weeks after I said no to babysit my nieces and nephews in hopes to hang out with friends. They didn't like my no, they didn't like my attitude. They had enough on their plates to deal with without adding my attitude and response to the mix.

The feeling of abandonment was nurtured when I found out 5 weeks before my father died that I was pregnant, and my mother was furious. My sister and my father were both supportive. I had just turned sixteen. I was able to understand my mother's anger, however, I also needed her to see the pain and fear that I was experiencing.

It was only five days after my father died that I started to bleed, and was taken to the hospital. There, they discovered that I was having a molar pregnancy, where the placenta takes over the uterus, essentially eating the embryo and still displaying all pregnancy symptoms. I stayed in the hospital by myself.

The following day I was rushed to a neighboring hospital to have a D&C done to clear out my uterus by ambulance. I did that trip on my own too, further implanting the idea of having no one, and being completely isolated.

From there, my mother again kicked me out of the house, this time for good, as I didn't want to clean up the garage (and again, was giving attitude with my 'no'.)

These all sealed the deal for my Ego that I was abandoned, that I was alone, and that I had to face the world alone. In writing this now, I am able to see as well, where the 'people pleaser' has stemmed from, as my 'no' was always met with a stronger no, and the result was being alone.

So while I had focused a lot of my healing journey on healing the parts of me that were feeling abandoned by my father, I was completely blindsided to the fact that there was more abandonment that was surrounding the entire event, leading up to and leading away from it.

As an adult, I can see and understand that my parents were both just doing the best job that they knew how to do in that moment, and I hold no anger towards them, nor do I blame them for what their actions were. I am able to see that their own childhood wounds also helped to reflect the actions that they took towards me and against me. And that too, is okay.

When I reflect with my Ego though, I am able to see that this is where its own story began, where its anger and rage stem from, where its abandonment and fear where escalated and became a normal reaction to any experience that would trigger the idea of this all happening again.

Our Ego wants to protect us more than anything, which is where our triggers come into play.

If we only focus on the main events of our experiences, our blind spots may only inhibit us from working through the emotions that are connected to the implants of the triggers.

In the months leading up to, and following the death of my father, it was reiterated that:

a) If I used my voice to say no to anything, I would be abandoned.
b) The people that were to be 'safest' for me, were a source of my pain
c) My feelings were not 'safe' to express
d) My feelings were not valid. I would receive love if I was strong, and receive pain if I was not
e) It was better for me to 'go it alone' rather than depend on anyone for support, strength or love.

Through all of that, I became the person that said 'yes' when I wanted to say no. I became the person that readily abandoned herself, in the hopes of keeping everyone around her happy. In that, I became the 'go to' person for everyone else's feelings, regardless of how filled to the brim that I may have been feeling with my own. I became the safety for others and the danger for myself. I stopped trusting others, stopped trusting myself, and stopped trusting in God.

Bringing this into the light, after years of keeping it all buried was more painful than what I wanted to admit. I spent over seven weeks, feeling the emotions as they came up, one by one, flooding over me and sinking me lower and lower into a darkness I had tried so desperately to step away from for so long.

The issue with my stepfather prior to his surgery uncovered a deep pit of emotions, and left me raw and open. Rather than jumping right back into the relationship, with him, or my mother, I made a choice to be with the emotions that were coming up for me. I was done being a 'people pleaser', and done with being the one to blame for other people's inability to be with their own emotions.

I cried, I complained, I yelled, and I cried some more. I took journeys of listening to music from my younger years that spoke to the hurting parts of me, and cried harder. I talked to the people in my circle that were willing to listen to my anger and bitchiness. I repeated the stories over and over, until I got tired of hearing them.

I would hear from my sister that my mom was really sad that I wasn't talking to her yet, and for the first time, rather than feeling guilty, I simply said, 'I'm not ready to yet'.

In my heart, I was able to see that rushing this healing process would only reiterate the parts of me that were feeling abandoned. This time around, rather than 'getting over it', I had to listen to every word of my hurting parts, and love them. And for me, that meant I had to be okay with being with myself and my emotions, without the distraction or input of anyone else around me. My people-pleasing tendencies could only exist if I had other's emotions to take care of.

Funny enough, the very thing my Ego had been protecting me from feeling again (being alone) was the very thing that I needed in order to heal my heart. The more I was able to be with the emotions, and validate them in my experience, the less heavy the pain began to feel.

I would like to say that like magic, one day I woke up and felt better, and really, that is what happened, however there was a lot of uncovering, undoing and 'being with the emotions' that needed to happen first for the magic to happen. I can't reiterate enough that healing doesn't happen overnight… you have to be gentle and patient with yourself.

The day that I woke up feeling better, I messaged my sister and told her that I was ready now to talk to my mom. My mom and I made plans for the following Saturday to meet a local coffee shop and just talk.

I was a basket of nerves leading up to it. I wasn't sure what to expect, and I could feel my Ego trying to work overtime to come up with some worst case scenarios.

Ideally, I wanted my mom to admit that my step father's actions were wrong, that I had a right to stand up for myself, and that she was sorry to put me in that position.

Instead, she told me that she didn't understand (her go to for big emotional things) why I wouldn't talk to her, or why I was so upset. She told me that I reacted with the same anger that I did when my father was dying. She didn't believe that she had done anything wrong, and couldn't understand why I was punishing her.

Now, if that had been seven weeks prior, I most

likely would have been triggered all over again, feeling as though I was not being heard, that my feelings were invalidated, that she didn't care, that her emotions were more important than my own.

But on that particular day, I heard her words, and felt the triggers inside of my body. I heard the voice of my Ego in my mind, and grabbed hold of them with my heart and held them, whispering silently to myself that I validated my feelings, that I loved myself for feeling the way that I was feeling, that I was safe to feel scared, and hurt. In doing that, the triggers became pieces of light in our conversation.

I was able to see that the blind spots that I had kept hidden for so long were also blind spots for my mom's experiences as well. Her focus was also on the main events, using the main events as the reason for her own behaviors and emotions, and at the same time, using me as the blame for why I should have reacted differently.

A person can only meet you at the level of truth that they have been able to meet themselves.

By meeting myself at this deeper level, and taking responsibility for my own emotions regarding all of the events, both the big and small, I no longer needed validation from my mom that my feelings were enough, that my voice mattered, or that she heard the pain that I was experiencing.

That responsibility became my own; and in that, my healing became my own as well.

By looking at my blind spots in my healing journey, I was able to uncover one of the most profound healing experiences to date for myself.

The blind spots, while small, were extremely mighty in reiterating the stories that I had been telling myself and believing about myself for so long. By uncovering them, and bringing them the voice that they had been needing all along, I was able to take my power back, and claim the healing that I had been longing for.

Heart Work

Take some time to reflect on the main events of your life. Write down the details of each and the emotions that are connected to them.

Now look at the blind spots that led up to the main event, and the after math of the blind spots leading away from the event.

What are the emotions that are connected, or similar in the main event and the blind spots?

What beliefs did you receive from the blind spots?

How are those beliefs connected to what you are feeling stuck in now?

Chapter # 12

Boundaries and the Empathic Heart

When we feel as though our ability to be safe, to be loved, heard, validated or seen are threatened, we often allow our triggers to start talking, even if we are aware that we may not be reacting in a way that we should be.

Often our triggers react when our boundaries have been long forgotten, and we feel as though we are the victim to someone else's behavior.

However, when you have firm boundaries in place for yourself, you create a space where your childhood experiences, your inner wounds, and your triggers all have a place to come together and say, 'Hey, no, that won't be accepted here'.

I was always sloppy with boundaries. I wanted to heal the world, and in that, make everyone else as comfortable as possible, regardless of how much I may have been suffering.

This was obvious in relationships, where I would often give more than I would receive; where I would agree to accept behavior that I truly didn't like; in work where I would over-pack my schedule to keep all of my clients happy with their wait times; sexual interactions that I wasn't in the mood for but would later relent to; and staying in relationships for much longer hoping to 'help the other person' be better.

As a result, I was often burnt out, frustrated and angry. At times, I was unable to figure out what my own emotions were as I was so used to feeling everyone else's. I had created the image of the 'perfect healer, the perfect mother, the perfect friend, and the perfect wife'.

Before I started to truly work with my Ego, it felt as though I was killing myself day in and day out, trying to 'be' all of these things that I thought were expected of me, sitting and watching life pass by on the sidelines, while feeling myself wither away in my own self-appointed cage.

However, as I started to work with my Ego, and connect deeper with my heart, I started to notice where someone else's emotions ended, and mine began; where others' expectations were extended, and where my own came into place.

At first, it wasn't easy. I would be aware of when my boundaries were being pushed, and at times shrink away and become smaller, allowing the boundary to be overstepped. At other times, I would be aware of a boundary being pushed, my feeling of safety being threatened and I would react with such an anger, a powerful force that was screaming, 'this voice matters!'

The funny thing about this was that when I would shrink myself down and allow others to overstep the boundaries, they would push me into a smaller ball, which only added to the bigger boundaries that they were overstepping. When I did lash out with anger, I would feel powerful in the moment, only to be left feeling smaller when it was all said and done.

I started to realize that I had no idea how to control my many emotions, and in that, I was just no different than the boundary breakers, as I was also breaking my own boundaries.

They say that what we don't process in our emotions will manifest itself in our bodies. My first symptom was breaking out in a rash; itchy little spots that would flare up in the sunlight, and looked nasty. My second symptom was extreme fatigue and lethargy that doctors weren't able to explain. My third symptom was (embarrassingly) a mix between constipation and an inability to my bowels, in the most inconvenient of times.

My body was the walking state of my emotions.

I had always thought that boundaries had to do with what other people were doing, however, it was only a story that I was telling myself, to let myself off the hook for the many ways that I wasn't honoring myself.

The more I turned inward and spoke with Kevin, this beautiful image of my Ego, the more I was able to see that my problems had nothing to do with anyone else, but rather everything to do with me, and how I was treating myself.

As I stated earlier, the first step to healing my own boundaries was giving myself permission to feel the way that I was feeling, regardless of the experience, or my judgement of the way that I was feeling. The more comfortable I was able to get with my own emotions, the clearer my own boundaries started to become.

We live in the day and age of the empath. For those who aren't aware, an empath is someone who can feel the energies in the room when they walk into a room, someone who is sensitive to others' emotions, and someone who can literally feel the emotions of others.

Chances are, the fact that you're reading this book, you're an empath.

The empath's biggest struggle tends to be feeling everyone else's shit, and doing what they can to make others' feel better from that shit. This often leaves the empath feeling worn out, burnt out, anxious and overwhelmed from social interactions or conflicts.

At a meditation retreat a few years ago, I found myself in a room with 200 other people, being led into a meditation to heal some of our deepest childhood wounds. We were guided to cry, to laugh, to scream, to wail, to yell, to *FEEL* what we couldn't feel when we were younger.

At first, I was feeling completely overwhelmed with the energies and the emotions that others were experiencing. I opened my eyes slightly to see who was screaming out in pain so desperately. It was a woman who had received a cancer diagnosis and ultimate death certificate only a few weeks prior to the retreat. I wanted to rush over to hug her.

But a voice came into my head and simply stated, 'Use her pain as a way to access your own'.

This was a new concept for me.

I had been so turned off from my own emotions that given the chance to dive deeper into them scared the shit out of me at such a core level.

As much as I wanted to rescue the woman from her pain, I realized that was my own desire to rescue myself from my own pain.

I stayed in the meditation, and uncovered so many emotions that were hidden so deep inside of me, using every wail, every cry, and every pounding fist in the room around me as another key to unlocking the pieces of my heart.

For the first time in as long as I could remember, I held the space for my own pain, in a room full of others' pain.

All of my life I had been the empath and sensitive soul who used other people's pain as a way to distract myself from my own; as an opportunity for me to step into a 'hero' role and 'save them' from whatever pain they were feeling.

In holding the space for my own emotions, I gave everyone else in the room permission as well, to also hold space for their own emotions. In that, we all healed at a deeper level than any of us had ever experienced before.

I can't say for certain, however, I don't believe that there was a dry eye in the room by the time the meditation was done.

They dismissed us for supper, and as I walked back to my hotel room, I felt the urge to use the bathroom. Squeezing my butt together, walking faster, and desperately praying to not let this happen here, I got about 2 steps from my hotel room before my bowels let out.

As I silently cursed my body, and peeled off my now soiled pants, stepping into the shower to rid myself of the remnants, I felt awash with such a shame and deep resentment towards my 30-something body that was failing me in the worst way possible.

Cleaned up, and ravenous for something to eat, I walked to the dining hall, where I found a seat beside a woman dressed very colorfully, her hair big, her personality even bigger.

She was talking about empaths and the psychic work that she does.

As I sat down, she smiled at me, turned back to her crowd and said, 'You know, the problem empaths have, is they don't realize that emotions are so personal. Picking up other people's emotions and carrying them as your own, is the same as walking into someone's house, finding all of their dirty underwear, and putting it on as their own.'

My mind flashed to my soiled underwear back in my hotel room that were now in the garbage, hidden from the world to see (and the poor cleaning ladies!).

I wouldn't want anyone to put those on.

I realized in that moment a very important lesson in creating boundaries in regards to my emotions, and the emotions of others.

What others are feeling is not my business to feel.

What I am feeling is no one else's to feel. We can be compassionate towards one another, we can hold space for one another, however, the moment we step in to feel in our bodies what the other person is experiencing, or step into save them from their pain, is the moment that we have crossed the boundary for ourselves, and for them.

This doesn't mean that we can't be compassionate for another person, have empathy or sympathy for what their experience is, or support them through their pain.

What this means, is we give others the space to BE where they are. We don't try to 'feel' what they are feeling, we don't bypass their emotions by telling them to think positively, and, unless they ask, we don't try to find a solution to whatever problem they may be having.

It is not our job to fix others. It is not our job to make sure they are 'feeling' a particular way (that is really more about our own personal level of comfort than theirs).

We are all capable of feeling a multitude of emotions. None of them good, none of them bad. Some just feel a lot more comfortable than others for us to express, or to watch others express.

I have spent most of my life being a big feeler. I feel all of the emotions, and express all of the emotions. Anger to grief, sadness to frustration, complete elation to complete despair. I can feel it all.

Over the years with my husband, I have noticed that he has a harder time expressing his emotions, and tends to go more so into the 'thinking' and logical part of his brain. On the other hand, I feel first and think later.

It was, what I thought, to be the perfect blend.

We have been dealing with some family matters for the past few years, which has highlighted both of these patterns for ourselves.

One of our children, due to their own traumas and childhood wounds when they were younger, are struggling a lot. Unfortunately, that means lying, stealing, screaming at us, and sneaking out in the middle of the night, drug and alcohol use, failing school, bringing knives and bb guns into the house, and uttering threats to the other kids in the house.

Every time another issue would stem up, I would go into my emotions and Jon would go into his thinking. I got frustrated with him for not expressing his emotions, he got frustrated with me for not understanding his logic. It was a tornado of back and forth, arguments of finding a solution to this out of control child, and misunderstandings. After a particular blow out, I told Jon we were either starting therapy, or I was done. I couldn't deal with the back and forth, the stress, the fear or the emotions any longer. It was in the therapy, that I started to realize that when shit hit the fan, I went into these big emotions, crying and expressing them loudly.

And every time I did that, Jon would shut down.

While I hadn't realized it, I was taking on Jon's emotions, as well as my own, and expressing them all. As time moved on, and issues continued to stem up, rather than expressing myself out loud, I started to work through the emotions on an internal level. In return, Jon started to get more vocal about his own frustrations, and while he didn't express him emotions in the same big ways that I did, he started to break the shell that he had put up around himself.

My empathic ways made it comfortable for him to not have to feel for himself.

The more I stepped back, and reminded myself that it was his emotions to feel, the calmer I began to feel, and the more he was able to start actually feeling what was inside of him.

There are two types of people in this world.... Those who express their emotions, and those who lock them all up.

Like all perceptions, we believe the way that we do it is the best way. Often because at some point we learned our own particular way to feel safest.

If you're frustrated with someone who is locking up their emotions, rather than wasting your energy trying to get them to open up, go within yourself to be with your own emotions.

If you're frustrated with someone who is extremely open with their emotions, rather than wasting your energy trying to get them to go within, bring your own emotions out into the open.

It does take effort.

There were days on end when my insides were churning with so many questions, wanting answers, wanting comfort or words or something. But eventually, holding the space for my own emotions and going within myself, gave Jon the safe space to bring his own emotions out into the open.

Chapter # 13

Creating Your Own Boundaries

As I mentioned earlier, boundaries were not my strong suit. I had people who would tell me that I needed to create better boundaries that I had to be clearer with my words and my expectations if I wanted others to listen.

I took it as a message that I wasn't doing a good enough job with myself, and that, ultimately, I had more work to do than the people that were overstepping the boundaries in the first place. And to that, I wanted to tell the world to fuck off. I was tired (from having my boundaries overstepped) and frustrated (again boundaries being overstepped) and I desperately wanted someone else to just point out to anyone who crossed my path what I was and wasn't willing to accept.

As much as I wanted the knight in shining armor to come and rescue me, it turned out that I was the knight in shining armor that I had been looking for all along.

It was highlighted to me this past summer how desperate I was for someone else to lead the way for me, to help me make the right decisions, to make sure that I didn't screw everything up.

My Ego and experience had taught me that if I didn't do things the right way, or what was 'expected of me' from society, people would leave and I would be the 'bad' person.

I had to call bullshit on myself, and the untruths that I had grabbed hold of throughout my life.

Many of us have them.

These ideas and expectations of how we are supposed to behave, respond, act and believe have been implemented since our birth.

The messages that I had received were:

- *Obey the rules that are in place, don't question them or face disappointment from those you want love from*
- *Say yes, even if at your own expense.*
- *Everyone else's needs are greater than your own.*
- *You are strong so you can take it*
- *Listen to outside authority, not your gut feeling*
- *Aim to please others*
- *Make yourself look good in society with outstanding behavior, outstanding acts of service, school grades, and being a good citizen*

Now understand, it's not as though my parents said these words to me directly. Just as I'm sure, your parents have never said these to you directly. However, we are quick to learn when we are children what gives us love, and what doesn't.

And so, we observe our parents reactions to our responses, and we begin to tailor our responses to what will give us love from our parents.

For myself, the messages I received made room for a messy relationship with boundaries, and trusting in my own inner gut feelings and intuitions.

And so, when I was faced with setting boundaries this past summer, it threw me into a tailspin as I tried to figure out the perfect way to respond to the situation at hand.

As I have spoken of already, we have had a lot of issues with my stepson. On this particular experience, he was caught stealing on a Thursday night. When caught, he began to yell and scream at me, and threw the stolen items at me. He then left the house in a storm, leaving Jon and I with the aftermath.

That Sunday, after a few days of not speaking or hearing from him, I received a message on Facebook from him, '*You need to come pick me up*'.

I saw the message come in, registered panic in my heart center, and closed the message away. About five minutes later, I got another message, this time just some question marks????

Again, I closed the message.

Everything in my body did not want to go and pick him up. I felt so deeply in my heart and my gut that this was a strong no.

And yet, a part of my Ego that was so attuned to ignoring the boundaries and pleasing everyone else started chattering away. *If I pick him up this time, maybe he will be nicer. Maybe this is a chance for us to heal whatever this shit is and has been. Maybe our family can be healed.*

Another message came in: *Hello? I asked for a ride.*

I closed it again.

Looking at Jon, I asked him, 'What do I do?'

Jon said, 'It's up to you. What do you want to do?'

I told him my dilemma. Everything in my body and heart was saying no, but the nagging thoughts were still there and very present. I was worried about creating a greater divide; about adding more anger to this already angry kid; about creating more havoc to an already chaotic year.

Rather than pointing out the way, Jon gave me the space and time to figure out the best answer for me.

I realized in that moment that I knew, and felt in my body, that a boundary would be crossed if I said to this command. What the boundary was, I was unclear about.

Instead of answering the messages that were

continuing to come in, I decided to lock myself up in my office to write out what my boundaries actually were. I had been people pleasing, strong, and doing the 'right' thing for so long that I wasn't even sure what this would look like.

It took some time, however, I was able to come up with some simple boundaries that covered all of the different facets of my life.

By looking at the times and areas in which I was most triggered, I was able to put together a blueprint of what my soul needed in that moment to most honor myself.

My boundaries were as follows:
- *I can be truthful and honest in all of my interactions and ask for the same from others. Based on their behavior I can choose to have less or more interaction with them.*
- *I can say no to people. My definite reasons for a 'no' include: lying, stealing, yelling at me or belittling me; name calling; not enough time, not enough notice, not enough energy/feeling too tired to be able to give my 100%, already working or have other responsibilities to attend to*
- *I can choose the hours I want to work. I can have set hours and respond within those time frames about new client appointments*
- *I can walk away from relationships and situations and opportunities. My definite reasons for this include: lying, cheating, stealing, abuse (mental, emotional, physical, sexual, spiritual), addictions, and fears/gut feelings to walk away without solid evidence as to why*
- *I will be responsible for my own triggers. I will not take responsibility for another person's triggers. When I am feeling triggered, I will identify my*

trigger, journal or meditate about it, hold space for my trigger and the emotions attached to it. I will respond to what comes forward in journaling and meditation. I will respond rather than react.
- *I will express my authentic truth in relationships, sexual relationships, careers and with strangers. I give myself permission to walk away from people and experiences that don't feel authentic*
- *I will speak my beliefs and views openly and respectfully while honoring other points of view. I will move toward deeper conversation. I give myself permission to turn away from any conversation that doesn't allow room for authentic expression, becomes abusive, dismissive or heated beyond comprehension.*

As I looked at my list of boundaries, I found that the fear-reaction that I had been having moments earlier was calming down. In that moment, I felt as though I was being heard for the first time, and it wasn't coming from someone outside of me, but rather that I was hearing my own voice for the first time, and rather than pushing it to the side to ensure everyone else was being taken care of, I was letting it take center stage.

I messaged my step son back.

Sorry. Due to my own personal boundaries, I won't be able to give you a ride. I need to honor myself and my emotions.

He replied right away, *what the fuck does that mean?*

It means that I am allowing myself to say no. It means that I am giving myself a choice from this day forward, to say no to anyone who hurts me, or oversteps my boundaries of how I want to be treated.

My hands and arms were shaking. I wasn't angry, I wasn't sad, or even frustrated. But my nervous system, that had been so highly trained to jump when someone said jump, was now being untrained from the 'known' and now acclimating to a new way of being.

He did respond again, laughing at the fact that I wouldn't give him a ride because he had stolen, and then threw in a sloppy apology, asking again for a ride.

This time, I just put my phone away.

If I waited for him to respect my new-found boundaries and the freedom I was experiencing, I would never move forward. It wasn't his job to respect them. It was mine. The part of my boundaries that said, I can choose to walk away from a conversation came into play and I allowed it to be.

What I started to realize after having these boundaries written down on paper was that my Ego finally had a reference point to check in on. Rather than overreacting that a boundary got crossed, I was able to start recognizing when the situation was getting too close to the boundaries. In that, I found my voice, and expressed that I had to honor myself, whether it be my emotional, mental, physical or spiritual needs.

I didn't need to fight to be heard, I didn't need to throw a temper tantrum, or hide away in a corner. I could simply say, 'I have a boundary on that, and I need to honor myself right now'.

It was all the permission that I needed to be able to honor myself and stand in my truth.

Heart Work
Write down the messages you received as a child that told you how you had to behave in order to receive love.
How do those messages still show up today in how you react to situations?
What patterns do you notice within your own lack of boundaries?
What boundaries can you create for yourself? What do you need to give yourself permission to do, rather than going into panic to make the right choice?

Chapter # 14

Who Does It Belong To?

So often, we are not even aware of why we think, see, feel and do the things that we do.

This past year, my husband asked me if the next time we got mayonnaise we could get Hellman's, rather than Miracle Whip. As soon as he asked, two of my children piped up that they preferred Hellman's.

I replied that I would get Hellman's, although I had never tried it. My mom had always bought Miracle Whip, so that was just what I did. I didn't have a reason to, other than that's what I seen, and for whatever reason, whenever I was in a store to get mayo, I would cringe my nose at all of the other brands, and grab the Miracle Whip, even if it was the more expensive option.

This is only one small example of these thoughts and beliefs that we pick up on, that aren't necessarily right or wrong, but are still not our own.

This got me to questioning many things in my life. What was actually my truth, and what was a belief that I had picked up on somewhere along the way, without realizing that it didn't come from me?

Suddenly I was thinking of buying motorcycles, selling the house, and buying an albergue along the Camino de Santiago in Spain.

The more I revealed to myself what was not necessarily mine, the more freedom I began to feel in my body. Suddenly, all of the worries and fears around what society, my family, my friends, my kids and my husband might think were no longer weighing so heavily on me.

I realized that none of what any of us believe is

actually true. It's all a perception of a reality that we have created on the limited perceptions of our past.

If I wanted to connect with the truth of who I was, I was going to have to leave all of the old stories and experiences behind.

My truth was not hidden in a mayo jar, nor was it tucked away in the secrets of the past. My truth was not the limitations of my parents, the fears of my childhood, or the weight or shape of my body.

Giving myself a definition of my truth didn't seem possible. My truth was so much bigger than any of my experiences, memories, relationships and more.

My truth was unlimited.

My truth was so big that I couldn't even grasp it.

And that's a truth for all of us.

We come here to Earth, these magnificent souls, all wrapped up in the sweet little flesh of an infant. And the infant so willingly and openly trusts those around them, completely surrendering to these massive figures in their life to feed and clothe them, to nurture them. Sometimes it works out, and sometimes it doesn't.

Our parents, grandparents, teachers and educators are all teaching us based on what it is that they know to be true at any given moment. This means that there are times when they are teaching us from their own limitations, and belief systems, based on their own experiences, and the wounded parts of their own egos.

One of my favorite quotes growing up was, 'Aerodynamically the bumblebee can't fly, but it doesn't know that, so it goes on flying anyway'.

When I first read that, I thought, wow, how absolutely wonderful. Bumblebees don't know anything about aerodynamics at all, so they keep following their own truth to fly, and shatter the thoughts around what they should or shouldn't be able to do.

But here's the thing: the quote was stated in the 1920's. It wasn't until the 1980's that scientists were able to discover that they had been wrong about how aerodynamics work, and the bumblebee should in fact (and does) actually fly.

Now imagine for a moment that back in the 1920's the bumble bee, in its own feeling of inadequacy consulted with the scientists to see whether or not it could follow its own dreams to fly. And the scientists, from their own limiting thoughts, said, 'Sorry bud, we get that you want to fly, but if you do, science shows that you're just going to crash'.

Humanity would have died. We wouldn't have even made it to the 1980's to find out that the bumblebee could actually fly.

Let that sink in for a moment.

All of us are like the bumblebee, wanting to fly, wanting to create, wanting to pollenate the world. And yet, so many of consult with the scientists of our lives who don't have proof of us being able to follow our own dreams, and so we clip our wings, and start walking around, knowing that there is something more out there for us, but trusting in the voices outside of us.

All of these voices outside of us are wanting to protect us from being hurt. They have our safety in mind. They know what is true based on their own experiences, whether that's the perfect truth for us or not.

My seventeen year old son got his license this past year, and I have been appointed to be his driving instructor. I'm a nervous wreck sitting in the passenger side. All of my fears about being in an accident come to the forefront. But here's the thing: I'm completely aware that my son is a great driver. He is calm, he drives within the speed limit, and he follows the rules of the road. There is nothing at all that is telling me to be fearful. And yet I am.

On Christmas Eve, he had to work the closing shift. I drove to his workplace to pick him and his sister up as they were done around the same time. In true Christmas fashion, the roads were covered in fresh snow, and a bit slick. He had asked me earlier that day if he could drive home if the weather was good.

On the way to pick him up, I could hear my thoughts. I didn't want him to drive. I wanted to get home safely. It wasn't him that I didn't trust, but rather the other drivers. I didn't want to have a car accident on Christmas Eve.

When he came out to the van, I said to him, 'If you want to drive, you can. I am fearful right now because it is snowing. But you don't have to take responsibility for my fears. You can be the judge as to whether or not you feel safe enough to drive.'

He had almost slipped on his way across the parking lot so he decided at that point that he didn't feel safe enough to drive.

Fine by me.

Of course, he will have to learn how to drive in the winter. We live in Canada after all. In that moment though I had to give him a choice to make his own plan. If I simply stated that he couldn't drive because it was too miserable out, he may have received a message that he was not a good enough driver, or that driving in snow is scary.

My fears are mine to own. He will build up his own fears over time. We all do. I don't want to contribute to them, and now make a point of stating what is solely my own fears rather than the truth of what the experience is for someone else.

We all carry these fears that contribute to us staying in our smallness. Generation after generation has experienced a limitation in some form or another.

In the healing work I do, I work a lot with family patterns and traumas that are passed on from one generation to another. Like the blind spots that we talked about earlier in the book, the stories of our ancestors can contribute to us overlooking root causes of pain and limitations.

When we start to look beyond our own experience, we can often discover where our family's experiences have helped us to form an idea, or thought about our own experience.

When I started driving on my own, I was always deathly afraid of making a left hand turn. I would wait (much to the fury of the drivers behind me, I'm sure) until there were absolutely no vehicles to make sure that I wasn't T-boned. I felt as though this was surely the way that I was going to die.

I had been driving for about 18 years with this fear looming in the back of my mind. One day, when I approached an intersection to make a left hand turn, the familiar anxiety came forward.

Rather than allowing the anxiety to be there, I said out loud, 'Who's story is this anyway?'

Almost immediately I seen a flash of my grandfather. He had died many years earlier after being T-boned by a dump truck. While the impact didn't kill him, complications from internal bleeding resulted in his death. Going even further back in family history, I remembered that my grandfather's younger brother, Joe, was also killed after being T-boned while riding a motorcycle. While neither one of them were making a left hand turn (they were both going straight) the result was the same. They had both been impacted by another vehicle and death was the result.

It's been a little over three years since I had that 'flash of realization'. My fear was not my own. It belonged to my grandfather's story and his brother's story.

If we don't pay attention, history does continue to repeat itself. Whether we are aware of our ancestors' stories and experiences or not, we carry the memory of those experiences in our bloodline, just waiting for someone to heal it.

I had to start telling myself that my grandfather's story, and his brother's story were not my own every time I went to make a left hand turn. I had to tell my fear that while it had a right to be there in my body, that I was actually quite safe.

When these memories are held within the imprint of our DNA it can be difficult to see it as not being a part of our story, or to not act out the same way that our ancestors once did. Fortunately, though it's in our epigenetics to be formed this way (again to keep us as safe as possible) we have the ability to shift it, to bring light to what the stories have been and to prove to ourselves that we are not limited by our ancestors' experiences.

Just like bypassing our own experienced hurts and emotional wounds, bypassing our ancestors experience can keep us stuck in the same story, wondering what the hell it is that we are doing wrong.

What our parents, our grandparents and our ancestors were unable to heal, we bring forward with us into our lifetime, in hopes that we will eventually be able to break the cycle.

This is where we need to get really honest with ourselves about what their experience was. What emotions ran predominantly in the family? What were the experiences around relationships, health, healing, money and security? How many of your ancestors followed their own truth, and how many followed what was expected of them? How much shame was in the family for those who stepped out of the box? What were the main sources of pain?

By looking deeper into the family stories and experiences, you can start to discover that some of your own limiting thoughts and beliefs are not actually yours to carry, but rather belong to someone else in the family line, and are just begging to be healed.

A client came into my office one day, exhausted beyond measure. She was running three businesses, while also cooking three meals a day for her husband and three adult children (who no longer lived at home). She told me that she couldn't give herself a break, or a vacation, even though she was extremely tired. Taking a break for her felt scary. She explained, that while it seemed silly, she felt like she would die without having her schedule jamb-packed with things to do.

As we went through her intake for an Ohana Generational Healing session, we discovered the root of her problem with overdoing it.

Her maternal grandparents were survivors of the Holocaust. Her grandfather, a handy man, was put to work in the concentration camps, to fix fences, gates, and anything else that broke down. The client explained to me that the guards would tell him that if he did the work, he would keep himself and her grandmother alive. If he refused to do the work, they would kill him and his wife.

As she told me this, I understood so deeply that her overdoing of everything was a survival mechanism that started with her grandfather. He had to work his ass off in order for him and his wife to survive the concentration camp. And while my client didn't have the same experience as her grandfather, the story that was deeply rooted in her DNA gave the message that she must overdo it in order to survive.

I looked at her, sitting across the table from me and said to her, 'Do you see the pattern here?'

She shook her head no.

I explained to her, 'Your grandfather had to survive. He had to work, even when he didn't want to, to keep your grandmother and him alive. This story that you're telling yourself, that you must work extra hard in order to live, is not your story at all. It is the story of your grandfather. He was safe though. He survived the camp, and he came to Canada, with your grandmother, and they started their family together. They started their family and you exist now because of their safety and the hard work that he put in. You are safe now. You don't have to keep working so hard to survive'.

She looked at me like a deer caught in headlights as this new awareness formed in her body. She gasped and her whole body started to shake, as she began to cry out generations' worth of pain, of working hard, of surviving.

I held space for her as she cried. When the last tear spilled out, she looked at me and said, 'How did I not see this before? I feel so much lighter, like a burden is off my back. How could I not see the connection?'

Like many of us, she was completely unaware of the stories that ran through her veins, creating new stories, and adding to the limitations that she was carrying. Because we haven't experienced the story first hand, it can be harder to pin point where the belief or emotion is stemming from.

For most of our ancestors, survival was the only way.

There was no talk about mental health, emotions, or healing in general. Life was about surviving, and preparing for the next thing to survive. They did the best that they could with what they had at the time.

And now we can do better. We can break the cycles of pain that they carried by being honest with ourselves about what their experience was. We can break the cycles by sharing their stories and offering them love and forgiveness, compassion and understanding for what their experience was.

We can discover so much hidden in the walls of our family's experience, and in that, discover so much of our own truth (and theirs) that has been covered up by years of pain.

By asking ourselves who the story belongs to, we can start to discover what we have been carrying as untruths, what we have been carrying that doesn't serve us, and what we have been carrying that our ancestors didn't have a chance to heal.

And in that, we can bring ourselves, and our family's story back into the truth of who we are, building on the strength, the resiliency and the bravery that the generations before us have brought forward as well.

Heart Work
What irrational fears or behaviors do you carry that you haven't been able to break free of?
Are you able to see those fears or behaviors connected to someone in your family before you?

Chapter #15

The Greatest Love of All

As I spoke about in Chapter 4 (What's Love Got to Do with It), we have been shown through music, through movies, through romance novels and the like, since the beginning of time, that when we are in a relationship, we are whole, and when we are not in a relationship, we are broken.

The completion of a person seems to rest solely on their relationship status more so than anything else in life.

And yet, the only relationship that we are guaranteed from the time of our birth, until the time of our death, is the relationship that we have with ourselves.

And for many (myself included!) this is the first relationship that we overlook. We are beings that long for connection, that long for physical touch, and intimacy, and at the same time, we disconnect from ourselves, our physical body and any attempts of getting intimate with ourselves.

You are the most important person in your life. Just like I am my own most important person in my life. Yes, my husband, my kids, my sisters, my family, my friends… they are all important too. But without ME, my perception and relationship to them cannot exist.

The relationship you have with yourself is the most important relationship that you're ever going to have.

When we listen to our favorite love songs, we often think of a lover, a friend, a child or someone similar who has made an impact in our lives. Very rarely do we put the words to use for ourselves, or sing ourselves the sweet nothings that we so deserve.

During the breakdown of my marriage to my ex-husband, I booked a weekend off work (I was a waitress at the time) and took myself to Niagara Falls, Ontario for the weekend. Niagara Falls is a honeymoon destination for many, and that weekend, I wanted to make a commitment to myself, as I left the commitment that I had made to someone else.

It was a very broken time in my life, and my heart ached in every sense of the word, but it wasn't for the relationship that I was in the middle of losing. My heart was aching at the realization of the loss of myself over many, many years of pushing down my feelings, not speaking up, and being sure that everyone else was being taken care of. It felt as though I had wasted my entire life being something for everyone else, and never what I needed and wanted.

That weekend came as a shock to many around me. They couldn't understand how I could just go away for a weekend, and leave my husband at home to take care of the kids. They couldn't understand why a woman would need that time away, especially after she had asked for a divorce two weeks prior to.

For myself, I didn't give a shit what they said. All I knew was that I needed quiet, I needed time, and I needed to listen to this 'thing' inside of me that was appearing out of nowhere. Like the Soul Callings, this voice (which I later learned was my intuition and inner child showing itself to me) was leading me into new territory, and it was so unfamiliar that I couldn't find the words that I needed to express it to anyone.

It was one of my most favorite weekends to date. I had so many long baths, read books, ordered in room service, and went out to eat on my own. I visited the casino (and had a huge win!) and visited my very first metaphysical shop.

On my last morning there, I wrote down a vow to myself: *I take my own hand, in love and in trust, and vow to be faithful, honest and committed to my growth. I promise to listen to my heart and to follow through with the direction that I am given. I pledge to honor you, to hold you, and to love you from this day forward and always.*

Standing in front of the mirror, I looked at myself, not in the way that one does when they are fixing their hair, but rather in the way of someone seeing someone they love for the first time in a long time. I spoke the words to myself, and felt as my body tried to resist them, and my emotions began to bubble over.

I felt more alive than I ever had in the past. I felt like I was doing something for me, for the first time ever. I was reinvigorated, and ready to move forward with whatever life was going to bring forward for me. I felt like I could trust myself, and the calling that was happening inside of me, even though I was scared as shit and couldn't see what that might look like.

This new commitment to myself didn't come easy. There were months that lay ahead of that day when I made the commitment, that were filled with darkness, chaos, and self-hate. There were days when I wanted to give up on all of my dreams, and hopes for the future, and there were days when I would think that loving myself just wasn't worthy it anymore.

I resisted the love that I was offering to myself for the longest time, but as the hard edges around my heart started to smooth out, I became more and more accepting to receiving the love that I had to offer myself.

Self-love is the real key to living a happy, authentic life. Self-compassion is the main ingredient. Holding yourself accountable for your own actions and reactions, is the stuff that holds it all together.

There is so much emphasis put on finding the love of your life, when the entire time, the greatest love of your life is standing there in the reflection of the mirror.

The next time you listen to a love song, imagine singing it to yourself, hands on your heart, and really receiving the words that you are hearing (and hopefully singing) to yourself!

This practice is one of my favorites, when I am needing a reminder to be loving towards myself first, especially after I've messed up in some way, and Kevin is being extra loud.

If you are finding yourself struggling with singing this to yourself, or imagining giving this kind of love to yourself, imagine then that it's the Universe that is speaking to you, loving you and supporting you in all the ways that you desire.

I have learned that listening to music this way brings in a whole new meaning to almost every song that comes out. I often ask myself, if this were a love song from the Universe, what would its message be? If this was a love song to myself, would I be feeling more loved and supported?

For a full list of love songs for yourself, or from the Universe, look for the Truth or Trigger Love Songs to Self by Catherine Graham on Spotify, or follow this link:

https://open.spotify.com/playlist/2Y6luuoAbiRgAvU0c7yLLE?si=Yoex3g5QQw6mPnOknul59Q

It's important for us to remember as well that self-love, and viewing yourself as the most important person in your life is not an act of selfishness. For many of us, we have been taught that we must think of others first, that we must be giving, and loving and nurturing and kind. And this is all true. But if it comes from a place where it is hurting you, it is no longer kind, or giving, or loving or nurturing (no matter how much you may try to convince yourself that it is).

The act of loving yourself is saying to those around you, 'I love you all so much that I am going to put my own needs first so that I have more to give you'.

The act of loving yourself and speaking your truth is saying to those around you, 'I value you and respect you, and because of that, I need to honor who I am at my deepest of levels to show you how you can do the same'.

The act of loving yourself and saying no is saying to those around you, 'I love you and I respect you, however I also love myself and respect myself, so I will decline and allow you to see that you are capable of this as well, or we can come up with another solution together'.

The act of loving yourself is the greatest gift that you can give to yourself and to those around you. You are showing them how you want to be loved, while also giving them permission that they, too, are deserving of loving themselves.

At the end of the day, isn't that what we all have been looking for all along?

And there it was, reflecting back at us in the mirror, quietly showing us the way back to ourselves.

Chapter #16

Finding Your Truth

With a world that is so quick to tell you what you need to think, how you need to be, what you need to do in order to be accepted by society, it can be hard to know what your internal truth is. In fact, we are being so conditioned when we enter into this world, that the majority of our thoughts, beliefs and stories are what we have picked up from others. Having an original thought is actually not that common.

Who would you be without your mother's voice guiding you or reprimanding you? Who would you be without your father's fears and dreams? Who would you be without your peers influence? Who would you be without social media, the internet, or television? Who would you be without fictional stories and biographies? Who would you be if you let go of all of the stories, ideas, thoughts and limitations?

The answer is simple.

You would realize the infinite being that you are.

You already are the infinite being, and yet, the thoughts, limiting beliefs and stories that you carry, make you believe that there's something more, something better, something to be fixed, something to correct about who you are.

And yet, what if in this moment, you decided to tell yourself that you're actually perfect just the way that you are? What if you accepted the greatness that your Soul has come to Earth to experience, to create and exist in?

Our Souls are so much more than the physical experience, the physical body and the thoughts that come along with a mind that has been conditioned to believe that it needs to be more.

The Soul desires freedom, expression, love, creativity, guidance and connection. The Ego and the human-ness that we each are, has a desire for the material items... the beautiful house, the money, material items, and perfect boobs. This is the stuff that we can't carry forward with us. It all stays here on Earth, while the Soul travels onto its next lifetime, or to recreate with the Universal energies that created us in the first place.

This is the greatest conundrum to us humans. We are taught that in order to be successful in life, we need to get a good education; buy the car; have a perfect wedding; buy the house; have the nice things; have the perfect hair, clothes and body type; travel; have children; retire; have a retirement savings, etc. It's one big long list of collecting items and achievements that aren't ever asking, 'Is this what your Soul truly wants?'

None of these are bad things to have. You don't need to live an impoverished life with no real connections to others in order to be spiritual, or to live in your Truth.

The only real time that they are bad news is if it's not something that your Soul actually wants.

Retirement for example is not something that I am prepared for like I 'should' be at my age. I don't have the RRSP's that financial advisors would tell me to get. But here's the thing: I'm not worried. I don't plan on retiring. In fact, I look forward to carrying my work out in the world until I take my last breath. Sure, I may vacation more, rest longer, or take bigger breaks in between clients, but overall, I am wanting to do 'my work' until the very end.

I have two options to choose from: Choice A accepts the fact that my Soul desires to continue to do the work that I do until I can no longer. Choice B starts reiterating the failure that I have created in my life by not having a retirement plan in place.

While neither are 'right' or 'wrong', I'll tell you, following the Soul's calling, rather than the thought that I have fucked myself over, feels a hell of a lot lighter and more heart centered.

And yet, so often, when I meet with clients and friends, the conversation of struggles will be tainted by the 'shoulds' and comparisons of life.

One client was talking to me about a potential relationship. Her parents, and her friends all seen this man as being the client's ideal mate. He had a good, steady job, he was good looking enough (her words, not mine!), and was ready to give her the world.

However, she didn't feel the *spark* in her Soul. In fact, she felt kind of repulsed at the idea of being with him. She was worried about letting her parents and her friends down so was inquiring as to whether or not she should pursue him.

I could feel the struggle within her, and asked, 'Is this what your Soul wants?'

She started to cry. 'No,' she whispered, 'but I'm almost thirty, and my parents approve of him, and all of my friends are married and having children.'

'That's their story though, and perhaps what's highest for their Soul', I told her. 'What is it that your Soul wants more than him?'

She laughed. 'Everything!'

She continued, 'I want to travel. I want to go to Asia for a year. I have the money saved up. But everyone tells me it's such a waste of time, a waste of money. I don't know why I want to go, and I don't know what I will do when I'm there. I'm scared to do it'.

Again, the ideas and beliefs of those around her, was keeping her from listening to the calling of her Soul. Her own fears about following her truth was keeping her stuck, her own beliefs about what her role was to her family and friends (keeping them happier than she herself was) kept her stuck exactly where she was.

We talked some more, and I later received an email from her. She did go to Asia. She met and fell in love with a musician. They have two children together. He supports her and her own visions of what she's creating in the world, and she does the same for him.

And her family and friends that wanted to set her up with the ideal mate? They have told her that she's happier now than they had ever seen her.

The thing is, most of our loved ones, family and friends included, have the best of intentions for us.

And yet, the best of their intentions are also limited by their own experiences.

A friend who tried to open a business and failed, may warn you of the dangers of opening your own business. They think they are giving you good advice based on their experience, and yet, it's limiting your own vision for yourself.

A father who tells you that pursuing a career in art is a waste of time was actually a young artist once who got yelled at one too many times for being creative and playful. For him, it may feel scary to see the creative expression come forward from anyone, as he tries to protect his own inner hurt child.

As humans, connected with each other, we have to

be vigilant in catching on to when our own limited beliefs, stories and experiences are influencing what it is we are saying to others. Sometimes, we don't realize how much influence we may have on another's direction in life, and what dreams they decide to pursue or stop because of what we share. And sometimes, we are the dreamer, aspiring for something greater than we have ever experienced, and denying ourselves our own greatness because we continue to check in with people who are also living in the smallness of who they are.

The more we connect with our Ego, and allow ourselves to dive into a deeper understanding and awareness of where our own limitations come from, the more connected we can get to our Soul.

When we know that our Ego has felt rejected and alone, rather than agreeing with it, or saying no to any opportunity that brings up a fear of being rejected and alone, we can witness the Ego in the fear, and allow the Soul to shine on anyway.

When I was in grade eight, I received my very first writing folder as a gift from my parents. It was a black leather bag with a lock on it, and a strap for carrying it around with me. I loved that bag.

I loved writing, whether it be poetry or short stories. I always had something to say, and now I had a bag to keep all of the writings in, and extra pens and papers should I ever have the urge to start writing. (This of course was before everyone had laptops and cellphones to write things on).

One day, we all received a writing assignment. I don't remember if it was supposed to be a 'real life experience' that we wrote about, or a fictional story, however, I grabbed my real life experiences and turned them into a story of a thirteen year old girl, coming of age, and experiencing life for the first time. I wrote of my experiences in friendships and the first time I let a guy 'feel me up'. I wrote about fights with my parents, and a troubling fight I had with my mom. Although the assignment was to be five pages, I ended up writing over eighty pages. I was proud of myself, and proud of the story that 'my life' was creating.

One day, the class went on a field trip. I had been experiencing some bullying from a lot of the kids in the class, so rather than getting my parents to sign the permission slip, I told the teacher that I was unable to attend, and would rather stay back in the classroom than go on the trip.

There were three other students (who were also bullied) who had decided to stay back from the trip. We sat there all day, the four of us, working on various school assignments and chatting about irrelevant matters.

At one point, we decided to look through our teacher's binder. We were hoping to see our grades.

Under English, I found my name, and I was getting an 'A'. Beside the 'A', there was one line: *Excellent writing but weird.*

I felt such a rush of shame and humiliation wash over me. Forget the fact that she had said 'excellent writing'. All I took from it was that my writing was weird.

I couldn't confront her, or ask what she meant as I wasn't to be in her binder in the first place. And so, I allowed the seed to be planted that my writing was weird.

Every assignment that I wrote after that, all the way through high school, I questioned whether or not the writing was weird, and tried to make it as 'normal' as possible. I dulled down my shine trying to fit into her box.

When I sat down to write my first book, the thought

came back, 'Make it normal'. And then the second book, the same thing. With my third book, I thought, okay, time to break this, be a little bit more vulnerable. With the fourth book, the thought was still there, and yet this time, it had a bit of rebellion in it, saying, 'Fuck that, let's expose it all'.

And now here I sit, writing my fifth book, and just last week, as I was hearing that same story again playing on in my mind, it dawned on me: I won the writing award that year. It was an award that didn't previously exist. They created the award for me. The teacher said as much when she presented it to me.

Yet, I had spent 24 years of my life trying to write as 'normal' as possible, trying to eliminate any 'weirdness' that my writing contain.

I looked up the definition of weird just now.

The Cambridge Oxford Dictionary explains weird as *strange and different from anything natural or ordinary.* The word itself goes back to 900AD and comes from the word 'worth'. It was popularized with the story of Macbeth and the 'werde sisters' known as the 'Fates', which associated the word with divinity, and anything outside of the natural law of things.

I spent so long seeing the weird as a bad thing, when really, what she had said in her binder, was that I was anything but ordinary with my writing. Everything I have strived to do with my writing, with my work, with my family, was already a part of who I was back then.

Thirteen year old me was deeply hurt by the words and carried that story around for twenty four years. Thirty seven year old me sees and feels so much value in them. Thirteen year old me was insecure, and looking for any proof to stop my dreams. Thirty seven year old me is taking her power back, and creating her own story, weirdness and all.

I have no idea what my teacher meant with her remark. She may have intended it as a compliment, a side thought, or a criticism. What her intention was really has no bearing. It was my own internalizing of it that created it to be much bigger than it needed to be.

Our truth is something that only we can reveal.

While we can't stop others from offering their opinion, giving their thoughts, or expressing their concerns, only we can choose to grab what we want as our truth.

I spent so much of my life thinking that my writing wasn't good because of a written comment that I wasn't even supposed to see in the first place. The writing award at the end of grade eight was dismissed in my mind because I was holding on so tightly to what I had perceived as criticism.

So often, we grab hold of the most negative things we have heard, and claim those to be the truth, and dismiss what is good about who we are.

We are born into this world with all of the confidence in the world, even though we are born shitting ourselves and depending on others to take care of us. We color without questioning whether we are good enough, we dance without knowing what a beat is or what the latest TikTok trends are, we sing and laugh and play because it is what we are wanting to do. We trust our own inner knowing and listen to it, and follow its direction.

And then something switches. Rather than checking in with our own natural rhythms and abilities, we start to compare ourselves to others, we listen to our parents' fears and limitations, we invest in others criticism of who we are and how we are presenting ourselves to the world. We no longer check in with ourselves to see if it's the right thing for us. We want the world to accept us, and we are willing to give up on our own inner truth in order to get that.

When I was around eight years old, I started to write a story about a little girl who found a 'ghost' of herself in the woods. The two had been separated for quite some time, and their reunion was quite emotional in my mind. I listened to Roch Voisine's song, 'I'll Always Be There' on repeat as I wrote the story, and yet, I could never quite understand what it was that my mind was conjuring up.

Looking back now, I am able to see that the little girl that I was writing about was me. The ghost of the girl was my own inner truth, fading into the background as I tried to be more accepted by the world. Somehow, I knew at 8, that I was sacrificing a part of myself in order to fit in, to be enough, to be loved and to be accepted. And yet, my truth was showing me that it wasn't going anywhere. It was happy to sit in a dark forest for a bit, but reminding me that it would always be there.

Our truth is who we are before the world takes over. Our truth never goes away. Sometimes it's buried. Sometimes it's over looked. But it's always there, ready and waiting for us to listen.

A Dream about Kevin- January 2021

    I am back in the house. The dirty house. But it's not dirty any longer. The house is cleaned. The walls no longer soaking wet. The wall paper is pink, with yellow lines. It's not what I would choose but I like it. There is big windows, and a lot of light is coming in. There are plants. The air is fresh and clean.
    Sitting in a red chair over in the corner is Kevin. He has a bookshelf beside him, stacked to the top with books. He is looking out one of the windows.
    'So you came!' he says to me, as he stands up. He seems older, more mature. Perhaps wiser.
    I nod my head, and gesture at the space that is around us.
    'Looks like we finally got it all cleaned up' he laughs. 'I can't promise it will stay this way, but here's hoping!'
    I laugh too. I know it's hard to keep things perfect all of the time, but I feel the sense that together we will try.
    He tells me to close my eyes as he has a gift for me. I follow his instructions. When I open my eyes again, I am sitting in a chair, just like Kevin's, however mine is covered in circles of red, rather than just plain red.
    I tell him that it's beautiful.
    He looks at me, and smiles, and says, 'The circle is for our completion'.
    'We're not done though?' I state, half questioning, half stating a fact. His eyes keep looking at mine, and though his mouth is not moving, I can hear what he is saying. This love hate relationship between the two of us has now become one of love. The entirety of why we had to learn to work together is coming full circle, and rather than 'two of

us, fighting one another' we are simply one. The way it was intended to be all along.

Chapter # 17

Following The Soul's Calling

In a time when you can be anything, why not choose to be brave? To follow the heart callings and the Soul's directions? To unleash yourself from what your past experiences have been so that you can live fully in the now?

In her book, A Return to Love, Marianne Williamson says:

"Our deepest fear is not that we are inadequate. Our deepest fear is that we are powerful beyond measure. It is our light, not our darkness that most frightens us. We ask ourselves, 'Who am I to be brilliant, gorgeous, talented, fabulous?' Actually, who are you not to be? You are a child of God. You playing small does not serve the world. There is nothing enlightened about shrinking so that other people won't feel insecure around you. We are all meant to shine, as children do. We were born to make manifest the glory of God that is within us. It's not just in some of us; it's in everyone. And as we let our own light shine, we unconsciously give other people permission to do the same. As we are liberated from our own fear, our presence automatically liberates others."

We don't need permission from anyone to step into our light, to become everything that we have always wanted to be. Sometimes we get caught up, thinking, 'When the kids are older', 'When my husband's supportive' or 'When I get the degree/certificate/money' than I will follow my dream.

All we need is the dream. For something more than what we have in this moment. All we need is the idea or the possibility that there is something bigger, something greater for us out there than what our current experiences are. The moment we begin to settle is the moment we tell ourselves that we don't have permission to step away from our comfortability.

The Universe has had your back since day one, and while your experiences may have taught you to believe differently, there is a reason that you are still here today, still working on your own self-growth, and still hoping for something more.

If it wasn't possible, you wouldn't have thought of it in the first place.

So now we know it's possible, because you have the thought.

Who could you be without your limitations? Who could you be without the limitations of others? What could you become if you only followed the direction of what your Soul is showing you? What could the world become if you followed your inner truth, just once?

I have been driving for 22 years. In the 22 years, I have gone in the ditch twice during the winter. In the 22 years, I have driven through winter storms, squalls, blizzards, and on one particular day, through the worst snowstorm in Canadian history, with over four feet of snow falling.

When I go out driving in the winter, I am a bit nervous. I am aware it's because the snow makes everything a little bit less predictable. Not only do you have to mind your own vehicle, the snow drifts and potential of icy spots, you also have to mind the other vehicles on the road, and pay attention to the possibility of them spinning out of control as well.

My fear says, 'Don't go out driving today, it's snowing. Remember that one time you went in the ditch? Remember when you had to find someone to get someone to call a tow truck? Remember how scary it was?'

My Soul says, 'Yes, that was scary. But there's been so many trips that I have been completely safe. There have been so many times when I thought it was going to be horrible, and it turned out fine. There have been times when I have had to slow down, and tread carefully, but I still made it'.

Our fears can be funny like that. Regardless of the fact that there have been hundreds, if not thousands of trips that I have been completely safe, the fear of the 'one time' still shows up.

We have to ask ourselves, 'Is this my truth, or is this my trigger?'

A truth feels expansive in your body. You may feel as though your heart expands outwards or opens up. You may feel a strong yes! Or 'truth bumps' when something resonates so deeply in your body that you get goosebumps or chills through your entire being.

A truth is not tied to an objective, a goal, an outcome or financial stream. At the same time, when we follow our truth, the objectives, goals, outcomes and financial streams start to just fall into place, without effort.

A trigger often feels restrictive, or demanding on the body. A trigger can make the heart center feel panic, or for the mind to start to create hundreds of thoughts of 'what ifs' or 'don't do that's'. A trigger can make your heart race, your emotions boil up, your mouth dry, and your memories to go to different times and places where you may have felt the fear or sadness or anger before.

A trigger is tied to an objective, goal, outcome or financial stream. Someone who has not felt safe in a vehicle due to an accident, will most likely have the same sense of panic show up every time they go to get into a vehicle. The objective here is to stay safe, no matter what.

Our Souls do not need money (everything that we could ever want is already abundantly available to us). Our Ego though can feel a sense of belonging, success, love and validation from 'having enough money'.

Our society celebrates those with plentitudes of wealth, and looks down on those who don't have much, or who we label as 'unfortunate'. The Ego grabs a hold of that story, and creates the drive to be successful, to not be the 'unfortunate' one; no matter the cost of the mental, physical, emotional or spiritual health of the person trying to gain the material success.

Understand that this doesn't mean you can't have money, or that if you have money that you're in a place of Ego.

In fact, those who are following the callings of their heart and listening to their truth tend to struggle less with money and find a flow of abundance with what it is that they are creating and experiencing.

The difference here is that they are following the Soul calling, not because of the stream of money, but because they can't imagine themselves doing anything else in their life. The call of their Soul is so strong that they are not worried about the money, but rather about following the Soul Calling.

When we are operating from the Ego, we may find ourselves worried about how much we will get, whether we will have benefits, if it will pay off, and how many we will sell.

Our Soul shows us our Truth.

Our Ego shows us our Trigger.

When we listen to our Soul and the Truth that it brings forward, it's like having your own personalized Spotify play list, featuring all of your favorite songs and music that you just vibe to.

When we listen to our Ego and the Triggers that is brings forward, it is like having your own personalized Spotify play list, featuring all of the music that makes you cringe and all of the 'catchy tunes' that play on repeat in your mind even though you can't stand the song in the first place. It is the song that never ends!

So often our reason for not 'doing the thing' that our Soul is asking for is tied to the fear around money. We worry that we won't make enough, or that we will somehow lose out by getting away from the 'safe' job, and following what the Soul is calling us to do.

In my experience, following the Soul calling has only brought in more abundance, more opportunities, more excitement and more energy.

Before I started writing my first book, 'Woman to Woman, The Journey To Me', I was working at a call center for Capital One, answering calls from people who were unable to pay their credit card bills. My favorite part of the job was the training and the group of people that I trained with. After the training was done, and we had to actually deal with real life people over the phone, I felt myself being drained of energy, real fast, every day.

About a month into the job, I started to write on my lunch breaks. I was going through a lot in my personal life, and writing was a way for me to deal with the divorce, new relationship, and healing that I was trying to get through.

The pull that my Soul had at that time to keep on

writing was huge. Bigger than anything that I had ever experienced before in my life. I would return from my lunch break, and keep a notepad by me so I could write down any thoughts or 'ahas!' that came through while I was working.

Of course, answering calls and writing a book don't work well together.

After another month, of piecing my scraps together I heard loud and clear that I needed to quit the job, so that I could pursue the writing.

This did not make any sense. I was swimming in debt, I had three young children at home, and in a new relationship with a man who also had three children. We were looking for a new house to move into together. I had to pay for my divorce.

At the time, I wasn't even aware of intuitive nudges, or listening to Guides or anything like that.

All I knew was that I needed to get out of the building and away from the job FAST.

I walked up to my supervisor, and asked what I needed to do if I was no longer wanting the job.

The supervisor explained that in order to keep in 'good' with the company, I would be required to hand in a formal letter giving a 2 week quitting date. Or, if I was sure that I would never want the job again, I could quit on the spot.

I thanked him for the job opportunity, and said I was going to pack up my stuff.

My body was exhilarated as I packed up and walked out those doors, never to return again.

I had no idea how I was going to make money. I had no idea if I would ever finish the book that was starting to grow inside of me. I had no idea if anyone would even want to read the book, let alone buy it. I had no idea why the pull was so strong, or why it had to be at that exact moment. The only thing I did know was that my Soul had never spoken so loudly to me before that.

I had no experience in writing a book, and no formal training in 'proper writing technique' either. However, over the next few months I continued to write my thoughts down as I worked through my own pains and started my healing journey.

At one point, I sent a Facebook post I had written in a moment of inspiration to the local newspaper. It was well received by the editor, and published the day before Mothers' Day (the busiest day of the week in the newspaper world). That gave me the confidence that maybe, perhaps, I could actually write a book, and that maybe, perhaps, at least one person would read it.

My Ego would love to tell you that the book turned me into an overnight sensation, read by hundreds of thousands of people around the globe, and changed my life forever.

The truth though is that the book sold less than 500 copies, and I no longer offer it for sale. It was perfect at the time, as a budding author, as a budding healer, as a noob to the whole world of energies and transformation.

The truth is also that the writing of that book helped me to find my voice, helped me to articulate my thoughts around my experiences, and helped to build the confidence in myself that was near non-existent prior to that. The writing of that book opened me up to what was possible and could be possible for me. It helped me to start to envision a future that was beyond changing diapers, doing laundry and falling into bed exhausted. I had wanted to help people for a long time, and the book solidified that I could help people by simply showing up and expressing my own personal truths.

By allowing my Soul to lead the way, I received an abundance of healing and transformation for myself. By allowing my Soul to lead the way, I created a new foundation for what my life would become and the possibilities of what that could look like.

The Soul Callings just feel right, without any evidence that they will be right. They don't need to make any sense to anyone else, or even yourself. If you feel it in your body, you know it to be your truth.

My Soul Callings over the years have varied, and looked vastly different: create bath bombs; make candles; get a job in a retail store; buy this book now; go on this trip; give this person your money; do this vendor show even though it's not your target market; walk down this street rather than your regular one; call that person; water color paint; walk the Camino; go to church; go to bed, etc.

There is never any rhyme or reason as to why I should do the things in the moment, however, every single time I follow the Soul Callings, I am met with so many rewards, spiritually, mentally, emotionally and physically.

And when it no longer feels like a Soul Calling, and I choose to let it go, I am met again with so many rewards, spiritually, mentally, emotionally and physically.

We don't need to hold onto anything longer than we are meant to hold onto it. A lot of times, our Soul will get exactly what it needed to get, whether a new connection, a creative outlet, a new opportunity or a deeper sense of healing, and then it's ready to move on.

We have been taught to be committed, to stay in relationships, to hold on, no matter what.

But when timing is done, timing is done. It's just as beneficial to let things go as what it is to create new things. Just as we need to inhale and exhale with our breath, so too, do we need to inhale and exhale everything in life.

Sometimes in life, our Soul Callings are like the leaves on a tree, here for a season, and ready to be released through change, not because they are no longer worthy, but rather because they have provided us with exactly what we needed. Sometimes in life, our Soul Callings are like the roots of the tree, permanent, unseen, and yet providing the foundation for everything else that we grow to be. It's up to you to decide what your root is, and what your leaf is.

For myself, 'transforming' is the root of my Soul Callings. How the 'transforming' shows up is my leaves. It changes season to season, day to day, and dependent on the energy that I myself am in, and that those around me are in as well. Sometimes our leaves plant new trees to take root, and sometimes our leaves rot into the Earth to provide the nutrients to the soil to nurture the foundation of the trees.

Just like the natural cycle of life, the 'death' of what was, creates the path for something new to come forward.

Sometimes we get so tied down to what used to bring us joy, what used to bring us comfort and what used to bring us peace.

However, change is inevitable, and what used to be your highest calling, may no longer be your highest calling.

Just like your favorite jeans from high school used to fit perfectly, you've grown, you've changed, and what used to be comfortable, may now need to be forced on (with a pair of pliers to do the button up!)

And that's perfectly okay!

We are here to grow and change, as we discover who we are now, in this moment, and let go of who we have been in the past. The art of doing this allows us to expand beyond our previous limitations, so we can see just how much we are actually capable of (which is completely unlimited by the way!)

As we begin to discover our Soul Callings, we may start to see that much of what we have filled our lives with was never a Soul Calling, but rather a way to put a Band Aid over a trigger so we didn't have to feel the pain from it any longer.

For myself, I believed that my Soul Calling was in 'helping people'. I would do anything it took to help others on their own path. I was tied into a pattern of people pleasing, and more than anything else, I just wanted people to be happy with where they were in life.

It wasn't until these past few years that I realized that the 'helping people' was more Ego-based in an effort to please everyone else, and putting my own happiness and joy to the back burner, in order to answer the 'Soul Calling' that my Ego was telling me I was fulfilling.

I had to take a step back from everything that I was doing, and truly ask myself, 'What is it my Soul is wanting more than anything right now?'

And the answer was not in helping people.

The answer was 'Transformation'.

That was it. One word. That could be taken in so many different ways. However, I was able to see that my entire life had been dedicated to transformation, on a personal level, in my relationships, and in my work. The difference between transformation and helping people was transformation required a personal accountability for both myself, and those I was connected with, whereas helping people required one person to be in distress or chaos, and me to be the savior they were looking for. In the second scenario I couldn't be the person in distress, chaos or in need of help.

This was an 'Ego Calling' that had been exhausting me for years, but because I had mistaken it as my Soul's Calling, I had just ran with it. The Ego Calling though was filled with my deepest triggers: *Keep everyone else happy or else you will be abandoned; You can't ask for help or you will be hurt; You have to be the strong one as everyone else is crumbling down around you; If people don't listen to you they will die'.*

The Soul Calling though brought through my deepest truths: *Everyone is responsible for their own happiness, including you; stop abandoning yourself. Ask for help, and open yourself to receiving support, from the Universe, from your family, from your friends. You are put here together for a reason. It's okay to not be strong. It's okay to be afraid. It's okay to be sad and heart broken. It is okay to feel. You can do it alone or you can do it with others. Only you need to listen to you.*

You don't have to have all of the answers for what your Soul Calling is now, in this moment. Like I've said a few times, it's more about a discovery of self, rather than an absolute for everything that will ever be. The Soul Callings can change over time, as you yourself begin to change. You can have the answer today, and tomorrow be more lost, and a deeper clarity the following day.

We put so much pressure on ourselves to 'just get it right' and to have it 'all figured out'. Our greatest gift we can give ourselves is the permission to be curious, and to remain open to that curiosity, as we begin to follow the simple steps that our Soul is laying out for us.

We gain way more on the journey than we ever do the destination.

And yet, for many of us, we are so focused on the destination that we aren't able to enjoy the journey as we are on it. It's in hindsight that we are able to see how much value the actual journey added to our lives, and sometimes, the destination that we had made up to be such a grand deal in the first place, ends up being less invigorating than the journey itself.

Allow yourself to be, in this moment, connecting to what your Soul is calling you to do, no matter how big or small, no matter if it makes sense or not.

Take a piece of it, and try it out. Notice the sensations in your body, your mind and your spirit as you do just the little bit. If it feels great (maybe scary too) keep going. You never know what kind of magic your Soul is leading to. You just have to trust.

Heart Work:

Take some time to list out your Soul's Callings (the things that you just love and want to do more of in your life).

What has stopped you from following your Soul's Callings?

In what ways has your Ego shown up as a Soul Calling?

What do you hope to receive by following the Soul's Callings? Are any of these reasons connected to the triggers that you listed earlier in this book?

Chapter # 18

What Does Your Heart Say?

Since I began my own healing journey, and began to work with others to help them along on their own, I have been passionate about following the heart's calling.

At first, listening to my heart calling was from a very ego driven place.

I wanted to help people in the same ways that I had been able to help myself. I also wanted to be seen as successful. I wanted people to like me. I wanted to fit in. I wanted to be spiritual, but not so spiritual that my not-spiritual friends and family would no longer speak to me.

I was very much driven by the idea of what my 'good work' would do in the world and how the world would view me because of what I was or wasn't doing. With this in mind, I would often hold myself back, afraid that if I spoke the entirety of my truth, or exposed too much authenticity, I would send people running for the hills.

When we are hidden behind a mask, however thick it may be, it feels easier if people are to reject us. We are in a place of rejecting ourselves as well.

To be in our full authenticity is scarier, however, when people reject us at that level, they are simply showing us that they are not in alignment with what our truth is.

I had spent a lot of my time listening to what I thought I should be doing and not a whole lot of time asking my heart what is was that it wanted to do.

As my relationship with Kevin continued to grow, and I began to let go of old thoughts, feelings and belief systems, I found my heart getting louder and louder, pointing me in new and exciting directions.

One question that I continued to come back to was 'How can I serve more people and make more money?'

The first time this question came forward, I was at a 'Make Your Mark' business event. As a part of the event, we had to do a meditation to see what direction our heart wanted us to go in, in order to take our business to the next level. There was a big push to take your business to a 6 figure income in less than six months, and while the idea of that was exciting, I was feeling more burnt out than I was wanting to come up with new ideas.

The image that I received was not what I was expecting. I envisioned myself in a bath, resting, surrounded by bubbles, soft music and candles lit everywhere. While this would help with the burn out that I was feeling, it really wasn't the best of business plans to get me to the six figure sales.

Months later, at the same transformational event that I first connected with Kevin, Kyle Cease had asked the entire audience, 'What is it that your heart wants more than anything?'

I remembered my 'bath vision' and tried to push it away. I wanted something more 'powerful' and more 'intense' than just a bath.

Just as I tried to resist, Kyle continued, 'Maybe you have been working your ass off for so long and now your heart just wants to rest'.

I don't know what words came after that, as I felt my heart sigh in relief, and tears flood forward. I was tired. I didn't want to change the world. I just wanted to rest. And as much as money would be nice, I just needed a fucking break.

I went home from that event with the determination to connect more with Kevin, and connect more with my heart. Rather than 'doing' I needed to learn to just 'be', words that I had often heard but didn't understand how to integrate into my life.

During one meditation, I heard my heart say, 'Try water color painting'.

It felt expansive in my body, but I had never done water color painting in my life. And while I enjoyed painting with acrylics, I was definitely not an artist. I tossed the idea to the side, but every once in a while it would come up again in meditation.

After about a month and a half of ignoring it, it came up again, and although I had no idea how it even made sense for me to do it, I went out and bought water color paints, brought them home, and promptly put them on my shelf.

Time and time again during meditation, I would get the simplest of messages: Try water color painting'.

After about six months of me denying this message, while out for a coffee with a friend, I told her how it kept coming up.

And in good friend fashion, she replied, 'So why don't you just fucking paint?'

I don't know why I hadn't, or what it was that I was resisting so much. When she said that to me, it was as though a light bulb had gone off in my head. I wrapped up our coffee date, went home and grabbed out the paints.

I had no idea what I was doing.

But it felt right.

The colors just flowed on the page, mixing together, vibrant and inviting. And my heart felt at peace... something I had not remembered feeling in a very long time.

I wasn't great by any means, and yet, just being in the flow of it was all that I needed.

A few days later, while putting things away, I started to flip through my attempts of painting when I heard, 'You can make an oracle deck'.

The thought of creating my own deck had crossed my mind before, but almost as an afterthought that was quickly brushed away. This time was different though.... I could feel a quickening in my heart, and an expansiveness through my body that I had never experienced before.

The next day, I sat down and started to write simple messages that could be put on each card. The process was quick and easy and the messages clear and to the point. The following month I started to paint each individual card, and the more I was painting the more connected to my body I became. I was in a flow like I had never experienced before.

Looking back I can see that this was the first time in my life that I created something that wasn't driven by a fear, or a doubt; it wasn't created with a thought of 'what if' or 'I hope they like it'. I was purely in my soul's expression of itself.

That was the birth of my 'Bitchslaps from the Universe Oracle Deck'.

I had no idea at the time of creation where it would lead, if anywhere at all. I had no idea at the time if anyone would like them, or resonate with them. All I knew was that I was just simply enjoying creating them.

I tell this story often, as the success that followed was nothing like I had ever tried to attain before then. Within a month of releasing them, they were being sold internationally. Almost three years later, and they are being retailed in stores across North America, and continue to be a thriving source of income for my business.

That's the thing with following the heart though. You ask the questions, such as, 'How can I make more money or take my business to the next level?' and then when you get a heart reply like, 'Paint with water colour' or 'have a bath' or 'go for lunch' it doesn't make a whole lot of sense to the mind.

We resist it because we are living from a place in our lives that was created by our own previous limiting thoughts. When we allow ourselves to drop down into our hearts and listen to the stillness that lives there, the heart shows us that we are not the limited beliefs we carry.

For myself, getting the answer 'paint with water color' seemed so impractical. And it was... for my mind. But my mind was also not aware of my souls' true desires... it was operating from a state of what it already knew to be true and safe.

My heart on the other hand was saying, *'Hey, if you do this one thing, even if just for a moment, you will expand your consciousness higher and the abundance that you seek will be following in ways that you can't even imagine'.*

Reflecting back to these moments has been the final proof that I needed to just start following my heart already. I had been tip toeing around it. Dipping a toe in and jumping back, dipping a few toes in and jumping back.

The day I decided to sit down and paint with water color was the day my heart got to be the leader. That was the day that Kevin was no longer an angry and loud voice in my head, but rather, he began to observe, to give playful advice and just allow the flow of creativity to be.

Just recently, I received another big message from my heart. 'Stop the one on one clients'. I had heard it three times in the past few years, however, it was usually after a long and trying day. This time, it showed up in the middle of a meditation.

Rather than humming and hawing over whether or not I should quit the one on one clients, like I did the with the water color painting, I allowed myself to sit with it for the night.

I realized that one of my greatest heart callings actually came from being in the flow of creativity. I loved to write, to sing, to paint, to create something new that wasn't in the world before me. The one on one clients, while deeply inspiring, and heartwarming were taking the time away from being able to follow the heart callings.

More than anything I wanted to continue to follow the heart callings; to live my life as authentically as possible.

And so, I chose to step away from working one on ones, without having a clue as to what was supposed to happen in its place. All I knew was that I had reached a fork at the road, the calling was loud! It was time to shift directions.

At the point of writing this, I am a week in to not booking one on one clients. I don't have any results to share with you, other than my heart feels free, and creativity is flowing in a way that it hasn't in a long time. I have received downloads for three different group events to create, and an idea for a fictional book that I now want to write. The results don't matter… answering the call is what matters.

Heart callings don't always make sense- not in the way the mind would like it to make sense. Instead, it feels different in the body…. This thing shows up, and it just *feels right.*

If we are at a place in our lives where we have worked through the emotions and limiting beliefs that were narratives of our broken ego, than we are able to step into each of the heart callings, taking direct action for our Soul.

By saying 'yes' to whatever is showing up from the place of your heart, you are giving your Soul permission to get bigger, to get louder, to be free of all previous restraints.

In the movie, The Shift, Wayne Dyer tells the story of 'The Death of Ivan Ilyich' by Leo Tolstoy, about a man who lives his entire life angry, and resentful because he hates his job and he hates his wife (she wanted him to have the career). At the end of the short story, as Ivan is laying there on his death bed, he looks at his wife and says, 'What if my whole life has been wrong?' and at that point passes away.

After reading that, Wayne wrote himself a note, 'Dear Wayne, Don't die with your music still inside you'.

Our hearts are calling us into action, every day. To step into a greater version of ourselves, to trust ourselves enough to take the chance, to break free of what has held us back, and to live a life that is full and authentic.

Our greatest fear is not in taking the action, but rather to live a life unfulfilled by not following the callings of our hearts.

We often get so committed to what has been comfortable for us. We stay in the job that sucks our soul out, but pays the bills or has a great pension. We stay in a relationship that is no longer valuable because we have already been in it for this long, so why look for something else?

We get so afraid of stepping out of the comfort zone, and yet, that is where we create our souls' greatest growth.

We are not here to stay comfortable. We are not here to keep doing the same old thing day after day. We are here to experience life at its fullest, to follow the heart's calls, no matter how great or small they may seem.

More than anything, our Soul just wants us to stand in the highest version of ourselves. When we follow that calling, we begin to step further into our authentic beingness. Whether your greatest heart calling is to paint, have a fucking nap, win a Nobel prize, or come out of the closet so to speak (spiritually or sexually) to those around you, whatever it is that your heart is showing you.... Do the thing!

A few years back, we had taken a trip to a local amusement park. Our youngest was graduating was kiddieland to the bigger rollercoasters in the park. His initial thought of going on the bigger rides was one of pure joy and excitement. However, waiting in line to get on the rides, often had his mind wandering and his Ego would become more present.

As the fears started to settle in, he would decide that he no longer wanted to go on the rollercoasters after all. He would then ask for us to turn around, and find a smaller ride to go on instead.

This became a cycle. We would get up to the roller coaster, he would change his mind, we would walk away, and then he would get hard on himself for not riding the big rollercoasters yet. (Funny how the same place that creates the fear for the changes is the same place that ridicules you when you believe it).

Eventually, I pulled him aside and said, 'I get that you're scared, and I love you for being scared. I get that this is tough, and I love you for being in this toughness with me. Whether you ride the rollercoaster or not is up to you, and whatever you choose, I am going to still love you. We can hang out in kiddie-land, or we can go on all of the big rides. It's all your choice.'

I went on, placing my hand on his heart, and looking

deep into his beautiful blue eyes, 'I know that you're scared, and I also know that you're capable. I love both of these parts of you. I am also scared when I get on rollercoasters, but then, when the ride starts, I am having so much fun that I forget about my fears and just have a great time. It's okay if we do this today, and it is okay if we don't do this today. The important thing is that we feel safe together, and that you feel loved right now'.

He gave me a big hug and we went and got on the rollercoaster. This time around, when the fears started to come up, I heard him saying to himself, 'It is okay that I am scared. I am safe and I am loved no matter what'.

Turns out, he loves rollercoasters, and as he learned that day, that being scared can be fun too.

The conversation we had that day about our fears and what they look and feel like in our bodies was an eye opener for myself as well. Looking at my son, I was able to see all of his potential, I imagine, in the same way the Universe sees it in you or I.

At the end of the day, the Universe doesn't really 'care' if you do the thing that it calling you or not (just like I didn't really 'care' if my son got on the rollercoaster or not). I did feel deeply inside though that if he were to give it a try, just once, that he would have the time of his life.

I imagine that this is what our Soul is like as well: the supportive parent, hearing the ego out, and saying, it's okay either way, but just know, if you say yes to this possibility, you are going to have the time of your life.

Sometimes the answer we are looking for is so simple we overlook it, thinking that 'that' can't be it. We like to overcomplicate things, and create a one hundred step plan that is so unachievable that we decide to not start in the first place.

We often wonder, 'Who am I?' and 'What is my life's purpose?', and the answer is simple:

You are your life's purpose. Healing your wounds, changing the narrative and stepping into the limitless being that you have always been, is your life's purpose. Following every heart calling, whether big or small, is your life's purpose.

As you answer each heart calling, you also begin to answer the question, 'Who am I'.

Spoiler alert: You are everything that your heart desires; you are the possibilities that you dream of; you are the answer that you have been waiting for.

Chapter #19

Seeing What Is Possible

The world is truly limitless in its offerings for what we can experience while we are incarnated here. We often get so caught up in our small stories, that we begin to see the world as being restrictive, rather than the unlimited potential that it is.

There is nothing in this world that you can't be, or have, or experience....everything is a possibility.

A few years back, I was challenged to write a list of one hundred possibilities, every day for seven days. A possibility was anything that I could possibly want to have happen or experience in my life. It didn't have to be 'true' as I knew it to be, nor did it have to make sense to anyone else.

At first, it was really tough. I had a few ideas of what I wanted to see, do and experience in life. But to come up with one hundred a day seemed next to impossible.

As I began writing the list, I was able to see that I had so many limitations that I had put on myself throughout the years. I could hear Kevin in the background, making the 'that's too hard' statements, or 'like that's going to happen' statements.

After I wrote the first list of one hundred possibilities, I found myself a little bit more alert during the day. After three days of writing a hundred possibilities, I found myself coming up with new ideas that I could add to my list the following day.

The cap of limitation that I had carried with me for so long was being removed, and I was able to see the world as a field of possibility, rather than a place that I had to push my way through, working hard, and achieving little.

I wrote one hundred possibilities every day for seven days. And then I committed to continuing to do it. And I wrote 84 lists. 8400 possibilities. 8400 ideas, inspirations, heart callings, and paths for me to take.

Somedays my possibilities were repeats. Somedays I surprised myself and wrote something that hadn't even entered my peripheral vision. Each day though, the truth of who I was, was being revealed through these lists and the callings that were being brought forward.

Of course, my Ego was still there, at times questioning whether it was truly possible, however, instead of telling it to shut up, I would just simply write the Ego's concerns as well.

So in one line, I might enter, 'It's totally possible that I am a New York Time's best-selling author' and in the next statement write, 'It's totally possible that I only sell five copies of the book and no one likes it'.

Now some may see that as being negative, or self-defeating, however, by the time I was writing these lists, I knew that my Ego needed as much of a voice as what my Heart did. If I were to resist it the way that I had in the past, I would only be adding to its fear. By allowing it to show up in the fear, in the limitations, I showed Kevin that, no matter what happened in the possibilities that we were going to be okay.

So often we are trying to protect ourselves from feeling failure, from feeling rejection, from feeling afraid, that we actually stop ourselves from doing the heart callings and stepping into our possibilities, which MAKES us feel the failure, rejection and fear that we were trying to prevent in the first place.

Your Ego doesn't magically disappear just because you start to look at the possibilities, or the limitlessness that you are. It is still there, and yet, showing it that you are okay, regardless of what happens, and allows this inner part of you to feel safe, no matter what you choose to do or not do.

In the time of writing these hundreds of possibilities, I have witnessed so many of them coming into fruition, including the finishing of this book.

From receiving a 'writers desk' like my Barbie's had when I was a kid, to university acceptances for my kids, holidays away, self-growth, home renovations, business projects, and healing deep emotions within myself, I was able to write the life that I am living and experiencing now.

It is easy for us to come up with excuses for why we can't do the things we want to do in life; to come up with reasons why we can't follow our heart's callings.

A client recently shared with me that she was really wanting to write a book. She had been wanting to write it since she was a teenager. Now a mom of two young girls, the desire was growing bigger, but she wasn't sure that she should, as she had bills to pay, a job to do and kids to raise.

Her biggest fear was that no one would read the book.

I pointed out to her that by her not writing it, no one was reading it anyway. The thing she feared the most was the same thing that she was creating in that moment by letting her Ego run the show.

I then asked her what her oldest daughter liked to do most. She told me that she loves to sing and dance. I asked her if her daughter is ever afraid of singing and dancing for others. She told me that she had been in the past, but her confidence had really started to grow, and she would often sing and dance in public, regardless of who was around.

Then I asked her if she would ever tell her daughter to stop singing and dancing in case no one would watch or listen to her.

Horror flashed over her face. 'Of course not!' she said. She was a good mom, who believed in every dream that her children had.

I pointed out to her that if she truly wanted to let her daughter know to follow this passion of hers that she herself would have to start following her own passion.

The child within my client, the young Ego that was so afraid of being rejected, needed to know that this woman would love and protect her as well, no matter what.

Quite often, the way we speak to our children is the way that we need to learn to speak to ourselves. The faith that we have in them, the trust that we have in their capability, the dreams we hold in our hearts to nurture for them….. These are all the ways that we need to be treating ourselves.

We can tell our children, 'I believe in you', however, if we are not mimicking a belief in ourselves that shows our children that it's okay to take chances, to follow our dreams, than we are only showing them their own limitations.

Kids truly believe anything that you tell them.

Your Ego is the same way.

Kids are eager to please their parents, wanting to receive love, and praise.

Your Ego is the same way.

You would never allow your kids to choose what was possible for you.

Don't allow yourself to let your Ego to choose what is possible for you, either. As the Ego is just the voice(s) of the child that you once were, know that it needs to be treated as such. With love. With respect. By listening. By not necessarily acting out based on what it is saying.

By allowing yourself to get in to the energy of what is possible for you, you break free of the limitations that you have held onto in the past, that have kept you in your comfort zone.

What I began to realize as I was doing the lists was that there was really nothing in this world that wasn't possible for me.

I could write a book. I could buy an albergue. I could run a marathon. I could own a retreat center. I could take a year off and travel. I could paint. I could heal relationships. I could heal myself. I could learn to fly a plane, or a helicopter, and I could pay off all of my debts, have lunch with Reece Witherspoon and write a movie, all in one day if that was what I chose.

It is not our triggers that define us. It is not our greatest fears or our biggest excuses.

It is our possibilities that define who we are… what we are capable of, and what our deepest truths are that are shining through.

Heart Work

Write a list of what is possible for you. Write as many as you can. Write multiple lists of what is possible for you. Write what you are wanting to create for yourself. Let your Ego talk too. Show your Ego that you are safe, regardless as to what possibilities come true or not.

Re-read your list every once in a while, and notice how many possibilities are now your reality.

Chapter #20

It's Time to Begin

Who you are at your core has never changed. You came into this world, absolutely perfect, beautiful and infinite. Your experiences clouded your idea of your limitlessness. But they didn't take them away.

An apple pie is still an apple pie, even when it's been sliced away from the rest of the apple pie. It's still just as whole, it's still just as good, it's still perfection.

You come from Source/God/Universe (whatever you want to call it). You are a slice of it. Which means you ARE it.

If you need to keep playing it small, and staying in your comfort zone, that's awesome. The seeds are planted. You will remember your limitlessness when you are ready.

If you're ready to take the leap, to love your Ego as you connect with your Soul, than it's time to begin. There has never been more perfect of a moment, more need for you, in all of your brilliance, than there is in this moment now.

The world needs you, and all of your glorious bits, and all of your messy bits. The world needs your voice, your experiences, your healing journey, your Ego and your Soul now more than ever.

Every moment, every experience that you have from this moment forward is a call to your heart asking you to listen, asking you to engage with whatever you are feeling, and asking you to show up with courage to listen to the truth that is vibrating through your body. Whether you perceive the experience as good or bad is up to you, however, know that each and every one of your experiences was designed to bring your heart out here in the spotlight so that you and the rest of the world can see just how fucking magnificent you are.

Your Ego's voice was never meant to keep you small. Safe, yes. But it's your job now, as the adult you, to show these wounded inner parts of you that you will be the safety, the love, the validation, and the voice that it has been longing for. It is your job now to listen to what these wounded parts of you are asking for, and to implement the changes that they are needing in order to receive the love and healing they desire.

And that may mean that you have to write that book that you've been pondering, while also holding and comforting your Ego; and it may mean that you're leaving that relationship that has been bogging you down for so long because you realize that even though you want to help, now you need to help yourself; or it may mean that you give yourself the chance to express yourself through art and creativity, to allow for more fun in your life.

Only you know what it is that your Triggers are showing you.

Only you know what it is that your Truth is pushing you towards.

Only you can give voice to the ego-thoughts, and only you can bring them comfort. Only you can listen to the Soul Callings and put them into action.

And now it's time to begin, to allow yourself to stand in your possibilities, to allow yourself to shine your light out in to the world, to use your voice, to follow your passions and to love the absolute fuck out of yourself, your dreams and your visions.

I am no expert by any means, but if there's one thing I know for sure, it's that we are all so blind to just how much we are capable of.

You may not be Oprah, or Gandhi, or your mother, or your second grade teacher. When you were being created, the Universe didn't want another Oprah, or Gandhi, your mother or your second grade teacher.

It wanted you and everything that you bring to the table.

Follow your Soul Calling. Know that the Universe believed in you so fucking much that it designed the entire earth around the visions that you are bringing forward, laying out an entire map and blueprint so that you would have the perfect path paved out to stand in your truth, to stand in your Soul and let your light shine.

As powerful as your Trigger may be, know that your Truth is so much more.

You are enough. You always have been. You have what it takes. You always have. Your voice is the voice that will change the world for at least one person, your heart is the love that will shift the world for at least one person, your imagination is the creativity that will make something new in this world.

I believe in you, and everything that you are bringing to the table. I believe in your visions, your heart, your Soul and your callings.

It's time for you to believe in you too.

Thank You

Like everything in life, nothing is possible without the love and support of others, to help you through to the next steps in your journey.

This book is no exception. Over the past two years, from the idea of its conception, to the very last word written, I have so much gratitude in my heart... this book wouldn't be possible without you.

Jon, you were the one who manifested the entire idea of Kevin, and building a relationship with my Ego. Thank you for the support, for the love, and for holding space through my most vulnerable moments.

Janice and Stella, you give Kevin and me a place to speak our truth, to share our vulnerabilities, and always bring a laugh to the conversation.

Crissy, you have always been, and always will be my sounding board, the one who gets me to the core and loves me in all of my authenticity. Consider the horseback rides repaid.

My parents, who gave me the best of love that they could, while also holding their own inner wounds. I love you.

My children, who give me the best of love that they can, while witnessing me heal my own inner wounds. You remind me what it's like to be human, what it's like to be a child, and what it's like to be love in all of my interactions.

In no particular order, to all of these beautiful souls who have been a part of my journey for the past three years as I worked with Kevin and fell in love with my soul, while also allowing me to bear witness to your own: Christine, Sandy, Kathy, Mark, Elizabeth, Shawna, Megan, Vered, Jennifer, Kristy, Kyle, Paule, Jenn, Karen, Lucinda, Kirstie,

Angela, Carissa, Amy, Christina, Michelle, Patricia, Lorena, Max, Sherry, Taryn, Tami, Jessica, Kirstie, Jean, Sara, George, Colleen, Daren, Renee, Sylvia, Jocelyn, Dee, Natascha, Aoife, Tammy, Breanna, Garrett, Rebecca, Brittany, Tammy Jo, Kelly and so many more that I'm sure I am missing. Every one of you have been a bit of the nurturing that this seed needed in order to grow. Thank you for showing up.

About the Author

Catherine Graham is an intuitive life coach, psychic medium and energy worker. Her no-nonsense approach in spirituality and her own spiritual growth and experiences helps Catherine to connect with many around the globe as they step into their own healing journey.

Catherine is a mom of 4 and step-mom of 3, and lives in Kitchener, Ontario with her husband and soul mate (not the Hollywood movie kind), Jon.

Catherine's life's work is to illuminate the path to oneself. Her work has been featured in Chicken Soup for the Soul: Divorce and Recovery. She has written 4 books, including Woman to Woman, The Journey to Me; Power Surge; A Journey into Fear and Naked Soul. Truth or Trigger is her 5th book.

Catherine has also created oracle decks for spiritual enlightenment: Bitchslaps from the Universe Oracle Deck; Journey within Oracle Deck and Journey the Fuck within Oracle Deck.

Catherine can be found on

Facebook.com/JourneyHealers7
Instagram: JourneyHealers
catherine@journeyhealers.com
www.journeyhealers.com

Made in the USA
Las Vegas, NV
14 January 2023